Backroads of
COLORADO

OVERLEAF: *The Sangre de Cristo Range*

RIGHT: *Entrance to abandoned house in the ghost town of Como*

Backroads of
COLORADO

by Boyd & Barbara Norton

RAND McNALLY & COMPANY
CHICAGO · NEW YORK · SAN FRANCISCO

PHOTO CREDITS

Library of Congress, pp. 74, 125, 136, 184-185; Library, State Historical Society of Colorado, pp. 16-17, 23, 30, 35, 36-37, 53, 56-57, 72-73, 76, 101, 177; National Park Service, p. 195; State of Colorado, pp. 24-25, 28, 40, 47, 48, 50, 64, 83, 90-91, 92, 93, 165, 170.

All black-and-white photographs not listed above and all full-color photographs were taken by Boyd Norton.

Sketch-maps drawn by Gene Sharp, based on maps prepared by Paul Tiddens.

First paperback printing, 1979

Library of Congress Cataloging in Publication Data
Norton, Boyd.
    BACKROADS OF COLORADO.
      Bibliography: p.
      1. Colorado—Description and travel—1951-
2. Colorado—History—Miscellanea. 3. Norton, Boyd.
I. Norton, Barbara, joint author. II. Title.
F781.2.N67   978.8   77-6900
ISBN 0-528-81046-4 (Hardbound edition)
ISBN 0-528-88220-1 (Paperback edition)

I go about self-appointed duties
  Afoot or in the pickup
Driving cruelly rutted paths,

  Tracing out the boundary lines
That corral men the length of their lives.

R. J. Petrillo

To all those who love and care about
the backroads and cruelly rutted paths,
this book is respectively dedicated.

B. & B. N.

*Wagon wheel
on a farm near
Elbert*

*Canada jay, or
"camp robber"*

Contents

Wild flowers and aspen in the San Isabel National Forest

Introduction

TODAY'S MODERN INTERSTATE HIGHWAYS are a boon to the American traveler, making it fast and easy to get from Point A to Point B. Let's face it, we all use them and I'm no different, being as impatient as anyone else to get to that Point B. The trouble with Interstates is that they are boring, frustrating, and deceptive, in addition to being convenient. The tedium of mile after speeding mile is broken only by rest stops and exits for fuel, food, or lodging. But even these respites do little to alleviate the overall boredom. The frustration comes when you spot local features and landmarks that you'd like a closer look at, only to discover there is no handy escape from this linear imprisonment. By the time you do find an exit, your initial enthusiasm has usually waned. And, finally, it's easy to be fooled in your impressions of a given land when you view it over guardrails swishing by at 55 per. The real flavor of a place can only be gained by wandering leisurely, talking to people, smelling, feeling, tasting the land at close range and slow pace.

In short, Interstates may give us velocity, but only backroads can give us roots.

Ever since I moved to the Rockies nearly two decades ago, I've been a sucker for backroads. The obscure, unmarked lane—sometimes it's only two wheel ruts—winding off over the hill or out of sight through the forest is too much of a temptation for me to pass up. I *have* to find out where it goes and why. So with squealing brakes, a tight turn, and a cloud of dust, I'm off. Sometimes, after hours of teeth-rattling, bone-jarring travel, the road simply ends in the middle of nowhere, with no evidence as to why it existed to begin with. Other times the reward at the end of the long, slow journey is some special place. A secret lake. A magnificent view. An enchanted forest. Some exciting bit of history or prehistory. Even though I'm an ardent backpacker and wilderness fanatic, I must confess that some of my greatest personal discoveries were made from a vehicle, bouncing madly over a dirt road in the middle of terra incognita.

Right off I should point out that there are backroads and there are god-awful backroads in Colorado. The former are merely fun, the latter adventurous and often hair-raising. Many of them follow the original pathways of a century or more ago, their condition improved only a little—sometimes not at all—since then. I'd be rich by now if I'd been paid by the hour for all the time I've spent lost, stuck, or groaning interminably in low gear over some miserable rutted track. I should mention also that I do not own a four-wheel-drive vehicle. When the going gets that rough, I usually prefer to walk. Besides, feet are easier on the land where there are no roads. So the backroads described here are those we've driven ourselves, my wife Barbara and I, in our plain old garden-variety Dodge van. It can get stuck and mired every bit as easily as a standard car. However, it does have a good, high road-clearance, an essential feature for any vehicle to be used for extensive backroad driving in Colorado.

Not all the backroads are rough, unpaved tracks, and some of them may surprise you. For example, US Highway 6 used to be the main, heavily traveled route over the Continental Divide at Loveland Pass. With the completion of Interstate 70 and the Eisenhower Memorial Tunnel, the spectacular and very beautiful Loveland Pass route has been relegated to the

9

rank of a backroad, used by relatively few people. There are those of us, however, who prefer it to the modern highway.

But whether the route you plan to follow into the backcountry takes you over a paved highway or over a pair of wheel ruts, before taking off it is always advisable to make local inquiry as to the condition of the roads—especially in mountainous areas. It can save a lot of grief and backtracking. It's also a good idea to take along a shovel, a tool kit, a set of tire chains, and perhaps an extra fan belt. A jug or two of water and several extra cans of beans may also be reassuring items in case you find yourself stuck and benighted by a late or early season storm, as I have on occasion. And be sure the spare tire has air in it.

Backroads of Colorado is not intended to be a guidebook. What I hope to convey here is more in the way of inspiration—blended with some useful information, in essay-picture-map form—to seek real adventure, to explore and savor the Colorado backcountry as I have. The mini-tours described here by no means cover the entire state. It would take more than one lifetime to explore all the out-of-the-way places and backroads of Colorado. Besides, there are a few spots that I'm keeping secret. You may very well find these yourself, and if you do they'll be that much more special.

The mini-tours include a sampling of all that the Colorado landscape has to offer: prairie, in the Great Plains; desert, in the Colorado Plateau area; and mountain, in the High Country. Each is fascinating in its history and beauty. So I urge you to resist the temptation to spend all your time in the rugged mountain country and explore the state's other domains.

For purposes of this book, I've arbitrarily divided the state into three regions: the High Country, the Western Slopes, and the Great Plains. Coloradans call the entire section on the western side of the Continental Divide—including portions of the High Country and all of the Colorado Plateau—the Western Slopes, but here I've used the term to mean roughly the western third of Colorado from a line drawn north to south through Glenwood Springs. In general, the length of the traveling season is the determining factor for this arrangement.

Each region is covered separately, beginning with an introduction in which the physical features are described and the driving seasons explained. Bad weather can ruin your trip; at the very least it can take the fun out of it. You can't always foresee weather hazards, of course, but the general guidelines I've mentioned should be helpful.

Every mini-tour is mapped, and for orientation, there is also a full-page map of the state showing all the cities and the principal roads. If you would like to find other backroads on your own you can start by writing for the US Geological Survey maps available from the Department of the Interior Geological Survey Office, Denver Federal Center, West 6th Avenue and Kipling, Denver, Colorado 80225. Ask for a master index. Or, better yet, if you are passing through the Denver area, it's worth a side trip to visit the office and browse through the great collection of maps. From a personal standpoint, I find the National Topographic Maps—1:250,000 series—to be the most practical and useful.

As a final note, this book entitles you to a free membership in the SPB—the Society for the Preservation of Backroads. I suppose there's not much danger of changing some of the roads described here, but I'm always saddened when I return to a place and find that the heavy hand of progress has altered it detrimentally and often at an unnecessary expenditure of time, money, and energy. I like the idea that for the really adventurous there will always be out-of-the-way places difficult of access. Joseph Wood Krutch summed up the lure of the backroad perfectly: "Rough roads act as filters. The rougher the road, the finer the filter." Those who care will make it.

Backroads of
COLORADO

The High Country

THE HIGH COUNTRY IS, OF COURSE, the region for which Colorado is most famous. Rock-ribbed barriers thrust high into the deep blue sky. Snow. Tundra. Glaciated cirques and basins. Swift, brawling mountain streams. Forests of pine, spruce, and aspen. Clear, crisp air. Country still clean, pure, and wild.

Colorado is the highest of the 50 states, with 55 peaks soaring more than 14,000 feet above sea level. Alaska has taller mountains—Mount McKinley is almost 6,000 feet higher than Mount Elbert, Colorado's highest peak—but Colorado's average elevation is 6,800 feet, while Alaska's is only 1,900. The lowest point in Colorado is 3,350 feet above sea level, whereas parts of Alaska are at sea level. Colorado boasts a city—Leadville—that is almost two miles high. And Colorado's mountains, though dwarfed by Mount McKinley, are giants in comparison to those east of the Mississippi, where the highest point, Mount Mitchell in the Appalachians, rises only 6,684 feet above sea level.

About half the state lies within the Rockies. As you approach them from the eastern plains the mountains seem to form a continuous, impenetrable barrier. You soon learn, however, that there are numerous routes and passes allowing relatively easy traverse from east to west. You also discover that the Colorado Rockies are not a single chain of mountains at all, but a series of distinct ranges, sometimes interconnected, sometimes separated by wide valleys, plateaus, and vast high swales, or basins, appropriately called "parks" by early explorers. These grassy natural parks include the San Luis Valley, North Park, Middle Park, and South Park.

The backbone of Colorado's High Country forms part of the Continental Divide, which separates streams draining to the east from those draining to the west. The Divide runs through the state from north to south. Here accumulated waters flowing to the east reach the Gulf of Mexico by way of the Arkansas, the South Platte, and the Rio Grande. Drainage to the Pacific Ocean is through the Colorado River system.

Geologically the Rockies are considered young mountains. Though not all the ranges comprising the Rocky Mountain chain are the same age, most of those in Colorado are 60 to 70 million years old. There was no single, cataclysmic upthrust that formed these ranges. Instead, slow, intermittent movements of the earth's crust produced the folding and buckling that raised the bare rock, bedrock forms gradually higher over millennia of time. And while the restless earth raised ever so slowly, counterforces in the form of ice and water eroded and corroded these mountains, transporting the scourings grain by grain to the dis-

15

*Mosquito Pass,
northwest of
Fairplay*

tant plains and even more distant oceans. Glaciers during the last three ice ages sculpted and faceted many of the peaks into the sharp jagged shapes so noticeable in many places today.

The High Country is also the gold and silver country that lured hordes of fortune seekers to Colorado in the last century. Many of the backroads which wind through canyons and twist in tortuous switchbacks up ridges and over passes follow the paths made by the prospectors. A few of the roads are old railroad beds of now defunct lines that once brought passengers to long-gone mining towns and carried out ore. Obviously, this can be tough, axle-breaking country to drive in, but the grandeur of the scenery is worth it. You can also absorb some of the region's history in visiting the tumbledown buildings of old boomtowns now being reclaimed by the elements.

For all its outward ruggedness, this is delicate country. Many of the roads will lead you far above treeline and into the strange and beautiful world of alpine tundra. In July and August the display of wild flowers is nothing short of spectacular. But increased motorized mobility in recent decades has begun to leave its mark. Wheel ruts become scars that may last for centuries on the slow-healing tundra. Because of the harsh climate and short growing season, some species of alpine plants may take as long as two decades to germinate, grow, flower, and reproduce. So keep your vehicle on established roads and when hiking, stick to regular trails. Even in the forested lower elevations, serious damage can occur when vehicles are used thoughtlessly.

The season for traveling the backroads of the High Country is relatively short. Many, if not most, of them are open only during the summer months. And here, summer means July and August, occasionally part of September. There are year-to-year variations, however, so always inquire locally before heading off into unfamiliar territory. A particular road that is accessible most years by the first of July may, in winters of heavy snow, be impassable until mid-July.

Sudden changes in the weather can also be a problem in the High Country. Even on days that begin clear and cloudless, storms may move in by early or mid-afternoon. Rocky Mountain storms can be severe, often violent as evidenced by the tragic flash flood in Big Thompson Canyon that killed more than 130 people in 1976. Fortunately, such disasters are rare, but it is wise not to underestimate the potential dangers of mountain storms. When traveling the High Country, keep an eye on gathering cloud formations. The small, puffy white cumulus clouds represent no threat, but take heed when they begin to coalesce into big, convoluted and dark cumulonimbus, or thunderclouds. Unless your view is blocked by nearby peaks or ridges, you often have warning of an impending storm. Such storms usually move in from the west or southwest in most of Colorado's High Country.

What do you do when the weather turns bad? In general, avoid the high, open expanses above timberline. If you should be caught at high elevations during a severe storm, stay put. Driving rain or sleet or hail can make negotiating those tortuous roads extremely hazardous. Most of these storms are brief, and chances are that in an hour or so the sun will be shining again. Your car offers the best protection against lightning. If you can't get back to your vehicle, there are a few important precautions that will minimize danger from lightning: Stay off exposed ridges and high peaks. Separate yourself from any metal-framed packs by a reasonable distance. *Don't* seek shelter under a tree. Lie flat on the ground and stay there until the storm passes.

Most of Colorado's High Country is public land—mainly in national forests. For purposes of planning your own backroad trips in this area, contact the regional office of the US Forest Service, Denver Federal Center, Denver, Colorado 80225. Excellent maps are available free and show not only roads, but campgrounds and hiking trails as well.

*The North Fork
of Lake Creek*

THE SPANISH PEAKS

I LIKE this trip because it has a variety of things to offer—flat, arid country, stately old forests, interesting geology, mountain streams and wild flowers, alpine spectacles, scenic vistas, pleasant ranch country, and the legend of lost Spanish gold. It also has a rather abrupt elevation change—almost a vertical mile—in a relatively short distance, bringing you up to 11,000 feet and near timberline.

Take US Highway 160 at Walsenburg, drive west about 14 miles, then turn south onto Colorado Highway 12, which runs along the Cucharas River. (*Cuchara* in Spanish means "spoon," the name apparently applied here because of the concave shape of the valley where the stream originates.) To the south are West and East Spanish Peaks (13,623 and 12,669 feet in elevation respectively), twin mountains that stand away from the Culebra Range to the west. The Indians called them *Huajatolla,* or "breasts of the world." The Utes believed them to be the home of fearsome gods and avoided them.

The legend of lost Spanish gold goes back to 1541, when Coronado journeyed through southeastern Colorado. On his return to Mexico, he left three of his priests in northern New Mexico to spread Christianity among the Indians. One of those priests, Fray Juan de la Cruz, traveled north to Huajatolla when he heard the reports of rich Indian mines there. According to the legend, the priest found fabulous treasures, loaded his mules with as much gold as they could carry, and set out for New Mexico. He was never seen or heard from again. In the middle 1800s, stories of lost Spanish gold continued to trickle out of these mountains and were repeated in such places as Bent's Fort in the plains east of here, but thus far the rich mines—if they ever existed—remain hidden in the Spanish Peaks country.

This area has a decided Spanish flavor to it, as you'll note in passing through the town of La Veta, which lies at the foot of the two mountains. *La Veta* is Spanish for "the vein." In the early years of settlement, a vein of

*The Cucharas River
Valley and
the Spanish Peaks*

white mineral was crushed and used as whitewash for the adobe houses and buildings.

Soon the highway enters the southern extension of the San Isabel National Forest and you have a view of an unusual geological feature. On the flanks of the Spanish Peaks are tall fins, or walls, that run for miles up and down the foothills and bear a resemblance to those of the Great Wall of China. These entities are dikes, intrusive veins of hard, igneous rock that have remained behind while softer surrounding rock has been worn away.

Before long the road begins rising steeply and curving in ever-tighter switchbacks. At Cucharas Pass (elevation 9,994 feet) there's a gravel road to the left that leads to

*West Spanish
Peak*

the higher Apishapa Pass (elevation 11,005 feet). As you climb this road, there are stunning views to the west and southwest of the Culebra Range, perhaps the only large mountain range in Colorado that is not part of the national forests. (*Culebra*, incidentally, is Spanish for "snake.") Near Apishapa Pass, West Spanish Peak looms several thousand feet above you.

There's a picnic area at the top of the pass where I spent several hours roaming around amid stunted alpine fir and meadow flowers. Apishapa Pass isn't *quite* at timberline, but it's close. Few people realize that the elevation at which trees cease to grow depends on both climate and exposure. Sometimes it can vary a thousand feet or more on a single mountain, with the milder south-facing slope retaining trees higher than the harsher north slope. In Colorado, the average elevation of the timberline is about 11,000 feet, but in these southern mountains, where the climate is somewhat milder, it can be 12,000 feet or even higher. In some places in the colder northern Rockies, timberline is often as low as 9,000 feet in elevation.

An approaching thunderstorm forced me to move on. Rather than retracing my path, I continued down the east side of Apishapa Pass and was treated to magnificent views of rolling hills and prairie country far off to the southeast toward Raton Pass and New Mexico. Somewhere out there, I thought to myself, may be buried the treasure of Fray de la Cruz. But it would take several lifetimes to search those thousands of square miles.

Once more in the lowlands, the road winds through typical arid country where you'll again notice a strong Spanish influence in the architecture. One very strange thing about the area near Aguilar: someone spent an awful lot of time and energy nailing old license plates to road posts. There are miles and miles of them. About six miles south of Aguilar is the site of the "Ludlow Massacre," described next.

*The death pit
at Ludlow*

Colorado Sketch: LUDLOW

LUDLOW DOESN'T EXIST. It never did exist—as a town, that is. It was just one more watering stop on the Colorado and Southern Railroad, which transported coal from the Trinidad coalfields that lay between and to the west of Walsenburg and Trinidad. Almost no one outside of Colorado had even heard of it until April 20, 1914. Then it became famous—or infamous—in a hurry.

Life for a Colorado coal miner in 1913 was not pleasant. Even if he managed to work the average of 200 days and thus earn 700 dollars per year, the company was always there to take it back. There was the company house rental, the company store, the company health insurance. And the company levied charges for blacksmithing and explosives.

The miner had no rights at all. The company ruled every aspect of his life, from what teacher his children had, to what books he was allowed to read.

He worked under appalling safety conditions. Each and every accident, however, was ruled to be the fault of the miner. "If he were more careful, he wouldn't have been hurt." And he could expect no help from the local or state government. They were as tightly controlled by the Colorado Fuel and Iron Company as was the miner.

23

His only salvation was the union. And so, in spite of the beatings administered to union organizers by the thugs that were hired by the company, the secret United Mine Workers' membership list grew.

By September 1913 the coal miners had had enough. The union called for a strike and some 8,000 miners walked out. They moved their families out of the company towns on the mountain slopes to tent colonies on the plains and settled in for what was to become an excessively bitter and bloody struggle.

Ludlow was the largest of the tent colonies. Several incidents there served as an excuse to call out the Colorado National Guard, under the command of the vigorously anti-union General John Chase. By April the guard had made four raids on Ludlow.

No one really knows who started the battle that day after Easter, the miners or the guardsmen. For Patricia Valdez and her four children, Cedilano Costa and her two children, the two Pedregon children, and the three Petrucci children, it really didn't make much difference. Eleven of them suffocated in an underground pit (where they had taken refuge from the flying bullets) when the National Guardsmen burned the tent colony to the ground over their heads.

There were other deaths that day, at least 20, but the world was especially horrified by the deaths of the women and children. The press referred to the tragic incident as the "Ludlow Massacre."

The strike ended in December 1914. The miners, for all practical purposes, lost. In 1917 the United Mine Workers erected an imposing monument on the site of the death pit, but as the years went by everyone seemed to forget about the massacre.

Everyone that is except Mary Petrucci and Alcarita Pedregon, the only survivors of the death pit. And they would never forget.

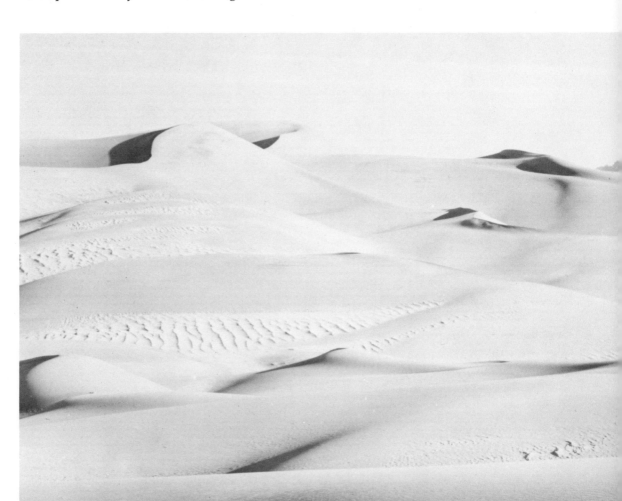

GREAT SAND DUNES NATIONAL MONUMENT

IN MY travels throughout the West, I've found several mountain valleys that have a special charm and beauty: Jackson Hole in Wyoming, the Bitterroot Valley of Montana, Teton Valley and Stanley Basin in Idaho. Ranked high among these is the San Luis Valley, which also happens to be the largest of the natural parks in the Colorado Rockies. Flanked by the rugged Sangre de Cristo Range on the east and by the San Juan and La Garita mountains on the west, this broad valley averages about 7,500 feet above sea level and is dotted with numerous ranches and farms. But to me its chief attraction and fascination is Great Sand Dunes National Monument, a ten-mile-long stretch of shifting, varicolored sands.

Sand dunes are obviously created by wind and aridity, and one thinks of them as characteristic of desert country like the Sahara or Death Valley. "But where did all that sand come from?" is probably the most

frequent question asked of rangers at Great Sand Dunes National Monument. It's not as foolish a question as you might suppose, for though the valley does seem somewhat dry, the many green farms and ranches belie its true arid nature. (Most of the farms are irrigated with water from deep wells.) It simply doesn't look like desert and sand dunes country. But it is. Average annual rainfall is less than ten inches here. (Precipitation of ten inches or less generally defines a desert.) And even though its high elevation makes it a cold desert in winter, it is a desert nonetheless.

But what about the sand? Where *did* it come from? And why is it piled up here in dunes that are almost 700 feet high at the eastern edge of the valley? In large part, the San Juan and La Garita mountains are responsible for the supply of finely ground rock which built the dunes. More than 10,000 years ago, during the last ice age, scouring

*Great Sand Dunes
National Monument*

25

ice chipped and eroded the bedrock of igneous formations in these mountains. With infinite slowness the rivers of ice moved downward from higher elevations, grinding and abrading as they went. Rushing streams continued the erosion process during and after the glaciation, transporting the sediment to the lowland valley. A large part of it was carried by the Rio Grande flowing through the southwest part of the San Luis Valley, and over eons of time the river gradually shifted southward, leaving dry, sandy streambeds behind.

Wind was the force that created the great dunes from this raw material. Strong southwesterly winds prevail here, and the sand has been transported across the valley to the present location of the dunes. The final factor for their creation was the great barrier of the Sangre de Cristo Range. The roaring winds, seeking the easiest flow, were funneled through gaps in the range, and as they raised up over the ramparts, their lessened velocity caused the sand to be dropped. Today, in the southeast corner of the San Luis Valley, about 57 square miles of dunes have been formed and are preserved as part of the National Park System.

To reach the area start at Walsenburg and take US Highway 160 west, then just beyond the town of Blanca turn north onto Colorado Highway 150, which heads directly to the monument. If you're coming from the north, you can take US Highway 285 over Poncha Pass (elevation 9,010 feet), then Colorado Highway 17 south toward Alamosa. You'll intersect a road a little north of Mosca that leads you east to the dunes. By either approach the road into the national monument is a dead end. Once there, however, you can leave the campground and take some short, easy hikes into diverse and fascinating country.

My favorite hike is north along Medano Creek, which flows along the east face of the great dunes. In May and June the creek is generally running well, but later in the summer it may be dry. As soon as I reach the creek I always take off my boots and walk barefoot in the ankle-deep water. You quickly discover that the dunes are not as completely sterile and lifeless as they appear from a distance. There are various kinds of small plants and grasses (in July there is a showy display of yellow sunflowers). In a few places cottonwood trees have taken root in the sand and seem to be holding their own somehow.

Medano Creek is an ecological interface between the arid dunes and the semi-arid foothills where grass, sage, juniper, and piñon pines grow profusely. If you slosh along here in early morning or at dusk, you're likely to see mule deer coming down to drink from the stream. A few miles north of the campground and on the east side of the creek is the "Ghost Forest," an area of dead ponderosa pines. Encroaching sand dunes have killed the trees, and the sleek, silvery remains look like surrealistic sculptures.

Another favorite hike is the trail to Mosca Pass, east of the Monument Headquarters and Campground, where you ascend through lusher montane vegetation such as aspen and spruce. A wagon trail used to cross over the pass and you can still see traces of the old tollhouse and stage station.

Be sure to spend time at the Visitor Center of Great Sand Dunes National Monument to learn about these and other hikes in the area. And don't venture too far off the beaten path. The dunes can be extremely disorienting—in fact, there are legends about sheep herds and wagon trains completely disappearing here.

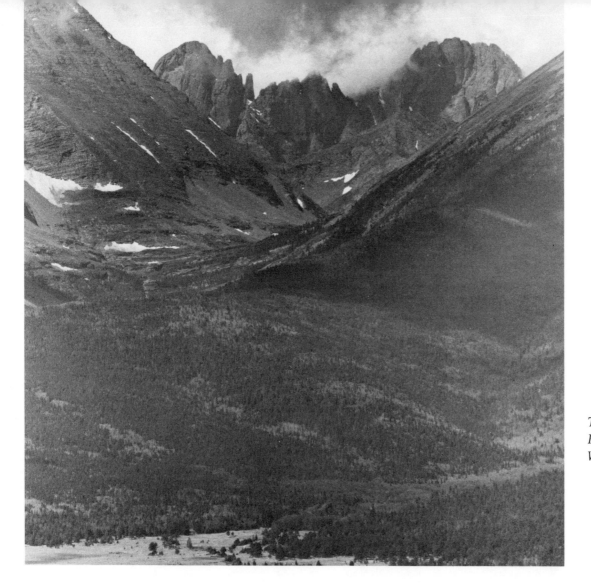

*The Sangre de Cristo
Range and the
Wet Mountain Valley*

THE WET MOUNTAIN VALLEY

ABOUT halfway between Canon City and Salida on US Highway 50, Colorado Highway 69 branches off to the south at the town of Texas Creek. This is a magnificent drive, for it parallels the scenic Sangre de Cristo Range to the west for many miles. (According to one story, the name *Sangre de Cristo*—Spanish for "Blood of Christ"—is derived from the utterance of a Spanish explorer when he saw a sunrise over the mountains.) This side of the Sangre de Cristos, known as the Wet Mountain Valley, is far less traveled than the San Luis Valley on the west, though no less spectacular. To the east are the Wet Mountains. Why the name *Wet*? Presumably some early explorers or trappers named them: after trekking over the hot, dry plains

east of Pueblo, they encountered their first storms and green slopes here, in these mountains that are now part of the eastern unit of the San Isabel National Forest.

About 20 miles south of Texas Creek, turn left at Westcliffe and follow Colorado Highway 96 east to Silver Cliff, a crumbling ruin of what was once a typical boomtown in the era of silver and gold mining. Incorporated in 1879, Silver Cliff became Colorado's third largest city within two years, but its population plummeted in the 1890s with the drop in silver prices. The abandoned mines are still in evidence along the hills and cliff faces. East of Silver Cliff, an unnumbered road leads south to Querida and Rosita, both now ghost towns also. You

27

can follow this road west to intersect Highway 69 again.

In continuing southeast on Highway 69 you somehow have the feeling of spacious, wide-open country even though there are ranges on either side of you. Several roads branch off and head toward US Forest Service campgrounds and small lakes tucked in the folds of the mountains.

As you leave the Sangre de Cristos farther behind and approach Walsenburg, you notice that there is an increasing Spanish flavor to the towns and ranches. At Farisita and Delcarbon I found some marvelous old adobe buildings and a few newer ones. You also discover that you've made a transition from high mountain valley to broad, open foothills of piñon pine and juniper.

*Old rooming
house in Rosita*

BLACK CANYON
OF THE
GUNNISON
NAT'L
MON.

CURECANTI

Blue Mesa Res.

Morrow Pt. Res.

Gunnison River

GUNNISON

4 mi.

N

50

50

To Montrose

NAT'L REC. AREA

149

Big Blue Creek

Big Blue Campground

Lake Fork

Uncompahgre Peak +

Henson Cr.

LAKE CITY

Slumgullion Pass

Divide

Continental

Lake Fork Rec. Area

Spring Creek Pass

La Garita Nat'l Wilderness

LA GARITA MTS.

CREEDE

WAGON WHEEL GAP

Rio Grande

149

To Del Norte

Rio Grande Reservoir

SOUTH FORK

160

SAN JUAN MTS.

Weminuche Nat'l Wilderness

HEADWATERS OF THE RIO GRANDE

NOT MANY people realize that the Rio Grande, or "Great River," which forms the border between the United States and Mexico, has its origins in the Colorado Rockies. Furthermore, the river here has a far different character than in the desert and canyon country of Texas.

About 16 miles west of Del Norte on US Highway 160, Colorado Highway 149 heads northwest from the little village of South Fork and follows the Rio Grande upstream. The river here is a typical mountain stream— broad, swift, shallow, and with excellent

Creede in boom days

trout fishing. A few miles from South Fork, the valley becomes hemmed in by cliffs of angular basaltic columns. At the place where the valley is especially narrow, you'll come to the town of Wagon Wheel Gap. The town apparently derived its name from the fact that in the early years a wagon was wrecked and abandoned here by prospectors fleeing attacking Indians. This area along the Rio Grande Valley has wonderful old cottonwood trees that blaze with color in the fall. It's especially nice to find a quiet place by the river and listen to the wind in the trees while basking in the warm autumn sun. This is dude ranch country, and pack trips can be arranged into the La Garita National Wilderness north of here or the Weminuche National Wilderness in the San Juan Mountains south of the valley.

Continuing on Highway 149 you come to the town of Creede, named for prospector Nicholas C. Creede, who discovered silver in 1890 and set off a stampede to the area. This is one of the most infamous boomtowns of the West's mining era. "There is no night in Creede," was a motto reflecting the rip-roaring atmosphere when miners poured into town at any time of day or night to wash away their cares in the numerous saloons. Today you can visit Ford's Saloon, built by Bob Ford, the man who shot Jesse James. Ford reputedly partook of his own wares quite frequently and on numerous occasions shot up the town in a drunken frenzy. But he died here as he lived, violently—shot in the back in his own saloon.

The setting for the town is magnificent, with cliffs rising almost 1,000 feet above the narrow valley. Creede's population reached a peak of 10,000 in the early 1890s and attracted a number of other notorious characters, among them Bat Masterson and Calamity Jane. The flashy and dapper Masterson was a faro dealer in a saloon owned by Soapy Smith, one of the more successful con men of the day.

Like all the boomtowns, Creede experienced the depletion of its ores and soon the whole lusty population pulled up stakes and moved on, following rumors of the newest strikes. Today the town is experiencing a new boom in the form of tourism, and with it a growth in population. The numerous shops and restaurants in restored old buildings do a thriving business.

About 15 miles west of Creede the road branches. Highway 149 heads north, and over the Continental Divide to Lake City (described next). The gravel road to the left leads west to the Rio Grande Reservoir, where there are several excellent US Forest Service campgrounds. At the end of the road, trails lead into the Weminuche wilderness, Colorado's largest preserved national wilderness. Here it's possible to follow the sparkling waters of the "Great River" to their very origins.

LAKE FORK AND LAKE CITY

WEST of Gunnison US Highway 50 runs into the Curecanti National Recreation Area. Just before you reach Blue Mesa Reservoir in the area, turn left on Colorado Highway 149. This first part of the trip is in dry, open sagebrush country, but gradually the land changes as you head south and southwest, climbing along low foothills. About 25 miles from the main highway the transition becomes abrupt as you pass between two high, steep cliffs known as "The Gate," which pinch off the valley of Lake Fork. Now the air becomes perfumed by spruce and pine rather than sagebrush and you get views of the high mountain country spreading out to the south.

Lake Fork is a beautiful stream, clean and pure. There are numerous places where you can pull off and walk down to the cold waters to try your hand with a fly rod or just loaf to the music of mountain waters.

About three miles south of "The Gate" is the turnoff for another of those great side trips. Watch for US Forest Service signs pointing the way to Big Blue Campground. This side road climbs steeply up from the valley of Lake Fork, twists through aspen forests and stands of Douglas fir. Topping a low pass, it descends into the drainage of Big Blue Creek which, like Lake Fork, drains north to the Gunnison River. Then the road wends through a beautiful, broad grassy

31

ABOVE: *The road to Big Blue Creek*

FACING PAGE: *Map of Colorado*

swale, brilliant green in early summer, and follows a stream dammed in numerous places by beaver. Bordering this green valley are dark spruce forests.

The road ends at the Forest Service campground. If you are not in a hurry to backtrack, this is a great place to camp and to explore on foot. The beaver dams alone are worth an afternoon's study, and if you sit alongside one at dusk you may be able to watch some of these industrious rodents going about their work.

Highway 149 continues to Lake City, once the center of considerable mining operations in the area. Today Lake City is best known for the story of Alferd Packer (see the sketch that follows) and for the many recreational activities available in the nearby Lake Fork Recreation Area. Unlike so many other towns of the boom and bust mining era, Lake City has retained some of its Victorian charm.

The road west of town follows Henson Creek and leads to the beginnings of trails into the Uncompahgre National Primitive Area to the north (wild areas being considered for designation as national wildernesses are officially labeled primitive areas). In a few miles the road begins to climb steeply and gets pretty rough, making it accessible only to four-wheel drives.

South of Lake City, Highway 149 starts the long climb up 11,300-foot-high Slumgullion Pass (the name is derived from a miner's stew popular in the area at one time). From the top of the pass you get a fantastic view of Colorado's high, wild country. To the northwest, dominating the landscape at an elevation of 14,314 feet, is Uncompahgre Peak. The road descends through forests, then climbs slightly to 10,901-foot-high Spring Creek Pass on the Continental Divide, with superb views of the San Juan Mountains and the Weminuche National Wilderness to the south. You are now in the upper drainage of the Rio Grande, described earlier.

COLORADO

Population: 2,209,596
(1970 census)
Area: 104,247 Sq. Miles
Capital: Denver

Cities and Towns

Akron	B-6
Alamosa	F-4
Antonito	F-4
Arvada	C-5
Aspen	D-3
Aurora	C-5
Boulder	C-5
Breckenridge	D-4
Brighton	C-5
Broadmoor	D-5
Brush	B-6
Buena Vista	D-4
Burlington	C-7
Canon City	D-5
Carbondale	D-3
Castle Rock	C-5
Central City	C-5
Cheyenne Wells	C-7
Colorado Sprs	D-5
Conejos	F-4
Cortez	F-2
Craig	B-2
Creede	E-3
Cripple Creek	D-5
Del Norte	E-4
Delta	D-2
Denver	C-5
Dove Creek	E-1
Durango	F-2
Eads	D-7
Eagle	D-3
Eaton	B-5
Englewood	C-5
Estes Park	C-4
Evergreen	C-5
Fairplay	D-4
Florence	D-5
Ft. Collins	B-5
Ft. Morgan	B-6
Fountain	D-5
Franktown	C-5
Fruita	D-1
Georgetown	C-4
Glenwood Sprs	D-3
Golden	C-5
Grand Junction	D-1
Greeley	B-5
Gunnison	D-3
Hasty	D-7
Holly	D-7
Holyoke	B-7
Hot Sulphur Sprs	C-4
Hugo	C-6
Julesburg	A-7
Kit Carson	D-7
Kiowa	C-5
La Jara	F-4
La Junta	E-6
Lafayette	C-5
Lakewood	C-5
Lamar	D-7
Las Animas	D-6
Leadville	D-4
Limon	C-6
Lincoln Park	D-5
Littleton	C-5
Longmont	C-5
Loveland	B-5
Lyons	C-5
Manitou Sprs	D-5
Meeker	C-2
Monte Vista	E-4
Montrose	D-2
Oak Creek	C-3
Ordway	D-6
Ouray	E-2
Pagosa Sprs	F-3
Paonia	D-2
Platteville	B-5
Pueblo	D-5
Rangely	C-1
Rifle	D-2
Rocky Ford	D-6
Saguache	E-4
Salida	D-4
San Luis	F-4
Silverton	E-2
Springfield	E-7
Steamboat Sprs	C-3
Sterling	B-6
Telluride	E-2
Trinidad	F-5
Walsenburg	E-5
Westcliffe	E-4
Wray	B-7
Yuma	B-7

Scale:
One inch equals approximately 42.4 miles
©RAND McNALLY & CO.   PRINTED IN U.S.A.

Colorado Sketch: ALFERD PACKER

THERE'S a college cafeteria named after him. At least one society, its members dedicated to serving their fellow man, bears his name, as does a wilderness cookbook. For a time—before people began making a fuss about it—the US Department of Agriculture cafeteria in Washington, D.C., was named in his honor. He was one of Colorado's most famous citizens. He was a cannibal.

Alferd Packer's story changed so many times no one can really be sure what happened that winter of 1874 near present-day Lake City. When he first staggered into the Los Piños Indian Agency on April 16, he said he had become separated from his five companions and had been wandering around in the snow, starving, for weeks. Fine. Things like that were always happening during Colorado's winters. But discrepancies in his story started to appear.

Well, he admitted, under more direct questioning, what actually happened was that they were starving to death, so when the oldest of the group died, they boiled up a bit of him to survive. One by one, the survivors ate the dead. Finally, there were three left alive. One of them shot another man and then went after Alferd. Naturally, Alferd had to kill him in self-defense.

35

Now, everyone was pretty upset about this latest confession. Killings were common in territorial Colorado. And a little self-defense could be forgiven. But cannibalism—never! Why, it just wasn't done.

So Alferd Packer was arrested, but before he could be tried, he escaped and was gone for nine years. Then he was recognized in Wyoming and brought back to Colorado for trial.

Forget the last story, he now said. This is the true one. This is how it began:

In Utah, Alferd Packer joined up with a group of 21 prospectors who were going to the Colorado goldfields. They darn near didn't make it. Luckily, they came upon the camp of Chief Ouray and his tribe of Utes who extended the hospitality of the camp to the prospectors for the winter. Packer and five others got itchy feet and left to push on to the goldfields. They had provisions for a week, but a snowstorm stopped them and they ran out of food. They even ate their moccasins. Finally, Packer left camp to see if he could find something to eat. When he returned, he saw one man cooking a piece of meat over the fire. The man attacked Packer so Packer had to kill him. It was only then that he saw the bodies of the others. And guess where that piece of meat came from? Packer was so hungry he couldn't help himself—he ate the cooked meat. He stayed there for about two months until he could get through the deep snow to the Indian agency.

The jury didn't like this story any better. He was convicted of manslaughter and sentenced to hang. Through a technicality, he was granted a retrial, but everyone knew how it would turn out. They didn't even bother to make a transcript of the proceedings.

Alferd Packer got 40 years, eight years for each victim. He served 15 years of the sentence until public sentiment forced the governor to pardon him. He died in 1906.

Right to the end he swore that he'd only killed one of his companions, not all of them. He never did deny that he'd eaten them.

CRESTED BUTTE AND GOTHIC

IT WAS a very hot summer day when I left Gunnison and headed north on Colorado Highway 135 toward Crested Butte. The land begins to look parched and brown around here in August. The first hay crop has been put up, and the second—moving in yellow waves before the hot, dry breeze—awaits cutting. The simmering highway has quicksilver puddles that disappear as you approach them—heat mirages. You are not aware of it, but the road climbs ever so slowly as you approach the town of Crested Butte, 8,909 feet above sea level. This was my first visit here, and right away I was struck by the resemblance to the area around Ketchum and Sun Valley in Idaho. Though the sun was still hot, the air here had an exhilarating brace to it.

Crested Butte is one of those picturesque mining towns that took on a new life as a ski resort. But it hasn't been spoiled by massive developments as so many other ski towns have. Fortunately, the frontier flavor has been retained in the original false-high-fronted store buildings, lovely old church, and stone-block jail.

The mining history of Crested Butte is rather prosaic, for it was coal, not gold, that spurred the establishment of the town in 1879. Within a few years a railroad from Gunnison ran to Crested Butte, carrying out the coal from the mines and bringing prospectors into the area. In the early 1880s gold and silver were discovered in the Elk Mountains to the north and soon the towns of Aspen and Ashcroft and Crystal were established. The Elk Mountains form a barrier that prevented easy travel between the Aspen area and Crested Butte, though mule trains did make the trip over high passes that are still accessible only on foot. Today about 71,000 acres of this range are preserved as the Maroon Bells-Snowmass National Wilderness.

Crested Butte

To Glenwood Springs

8 mi.

N

LEADVILLE

Roaring Fork River

ASPEN

82

Maroon Bells-Snowmass Nat'l Wilderness

+ N. Maroon Peak
+ Maroon Peak

Independence Pass

Arkansas River

24

ELK MOUNTAINS

MARBLE

CRYSTAL

ASHCROFT

Schofield Pass

Taylor Pass

Continental

Divide

GOTHIC

IRWIN

East River

Cottonwood Pass

BUENA VISTA

CRESTED BUTTE

Taylor Park Res.

306

135

Taylor River

TAYLOR PARK

TINCUP

Cumberland Pass

ALMONT

PITKIN

Waunita Pass

OHIO Cr.

GUNNISON

50

Quartz

WAUNITA HOT SPRINGS

PONCHA SPRINGS

I followed the road north from town leading to Gothic. The road winds along a steep hillside, and you can look down into the broad green valley formed by the East River. Across the valley are Maroon Peak and North Maroon Peak—both, as their names imply, maroon-colored. Gothic was a coal mining town with a population of several thousand in the early 1880s. Today only a few buildings remain. General Ulysses S. Grant visited here in the summer of 1880 before the railroad was completed. His party included Colorado's governor, Frederick W. Pitkin, and other state officials, and they traveled by mule team, with the former president doing most of the driving himself (he apparently distrusted anyone else at the reins). Later they headed into the mountains west of here to visit the booming town of Irwin, described later as part of the Kebler Pass trip.

From Gothic I had to backtrack, for the road now running northwest over Schofield Pass (elevation 10,707 feet) to Crystal and Marble is strictly for four-wheel-drive vehicles. In all, I found this a delightful trip and one that provides an unusually pleasant glimpse of Colorado mining history.

COTTONWOOD PASS

IF YOU are in the mood for a reasonably relaxed trip with fine scenery and good camping facilities along the way, this one is an excellent choice. Furthermore, if you should decide to stay longer than a day or two, you have the option of roaming several side roads in addition to the main Cottonwood Pass route. In all, the trip could easily be stretched into three or four days of leisurely exploration and camping.

Though Cottonwood Pass at 12,126 feet in elevation ranks among the highest in Colorado, the road to the top is excellent and easily traveled. Take Colorado Highway 306 west out of Buena Vista. This road is paved for the first several miles, then it becomes graveled as it climbs through aspen forests. For the last few miles to the top of the pass you ascend in wide, sweeping loops above timberline, where there are broad vistas of bare tundra and thick forest below. The summit is on the Continental Divide, and you may wish to stop here to explore some of this land above trees. In most years wild flowers will reach their peak during the first half of August, though some varieties, such as the alpine buttercup, blossom when there is still snow on the ground. It isn't at all uncommon to see the diminutive yellow flowers poking up through the last remaining inches of snow cover.

If you are here early enough in the year, just after the road is open and while snow still lies deep in protected pockets, you may observe the unusual phenomenon known as "pink," or "watermelon," snow. Responsible for this coloration are microscopic algae. Surrounding the chlorophyll center of the tiny organisms is a pink covering that scientists think protects them from excessive ultraviolet radiation at high altitudes. These microorganisms can survive in near-freezing temperatures.

Starting down the west side of Cottonwood Pass, you have distant views of Taylor Park Reservoir and Taylor Park, the latter a mountain-rimmed valley. Before the road was built over Independence Pass north of here, Highway 306 was one of the main supply routes to the mining camps of Aspen and Ashcroft. From Taylor Park the original road headed northwest, then climbed the rugged 12,400-foot-high Taylor Pass before descending into the Roaring Fork Valley. Even with today's four-wheel drives, the ride over Taylor Pass is rough, slow, and bone-jarring.

At the village of Taylor Park you can continue west, descending into the narrow gorge cut by the Taylor River, to the intersection of Colorado Highway 135 at Almont. To your right is Crested Butte. To the left is Gunnison.

Or, just east of the village of Taylor Park you can head south to the little town of Tincup (presumably named by an early miner who panned gold with his tin cup). From Tincup the road climbs steeply over Cumberland Pass (elevation 12,000 feet) before dropping down into the old mining town of Pitkin. Here you can either continue over 10,303-foot-high Waunita Pass to Waunita Hot Springs, or head down Quartz Creek to still another mining town, Ohio. Either way you'll eventually intersect US Highway 50 east of Gunnison. From the time you leave Buena Vista, you have about a dozen US Forest Service campgrounds to choose from along the Cottonwood Pass road, in Taylor Park, the Taylor River canyon, and the Pitkin-Tincup area.

Church in Tincup

N

8 mi.

CARBONDALE

133

Crystal River

82

REDSTONE

McClure Pass

PLACITA

MARBLE

Paonia Res.

Anthracite Cr.

Marcellina Mtn.

IRWIN

Kebler Pass

CRESTED BUTTE

PAONIA

Gunnison River

133

North Fork

Coal Creek

Lost Lake

Ohio Pass

Mt. Gunnison

West Elk Nat'l Wilderness

Ohio Creek

To Delta

W E S T   E L K   M T S.

West Elk Peak

To Gunnison

PAONIA TO McCLURE PASS

THE TOWN of Paonia is off a little-traveled but lovely road, Colorado Highway 133. It's a good place to start this trip, and the best time is in late summer, for there are numerous orchards and roadside stands that sell the succulent fruits (peaches, apples, apricots, and pears) grown in the valley of the North Fork of the Gunnison River between Paonia and Delta to the west. This is also coal mining country, although many of the mines have closed. You wonder about the incongruity of the dirty mines and a town named for peony flowers. (It was first called Peonia, but later corrupted by the post office to Paonia.) There is a fine view southeast across this agricultural valley to the West Elk Mountains, with 12,719-foot-high Mount Gunnison the most prominent peak.

Northeast of the town, Highway 133 climbs gradually up past the dam forming Paonia Reservoir. This man-made lake seems to be perennially low, with long mud flats exposed—hardly an invitation for recreational activities. However, as the road heads north beyond the reservoir, it begins to pass through thick aspen forests, and the land takes on a more montane character.

There is a decided Old West flavor to Highway 133 beyond Paonia Reservoir. Several ranches lie in the creek-fed valleys, and the road winds uphill and down, edged with barbed-wire fences held in place by gnarled old posts. Around one of the bends you are likely to encounter a cowhand urging a herd of cattle along the dusty road.

The last haul up to McClure Pass starts in a dry, dusty valley and goes through several fascinating biological transitions. Along the stream course are cottonwood trees, with sagebrush growing on the hillsides. The elevation is slightly over 7,000 feet. As the road climbs in slow, winding curves, you enter the zone of Gambel oak, or scrub oak, which has the typical lobed leaves and acorns of larger species of oak trees but grows as dense, tangled stands rarely over eight or nine feet tall. This tough tangle of brush is sometimes so dense that large animals cannot penetrate it. Scrub oak has always been the curse of the cowboy when calves wandered off into it, for it is virtually impossible to ride a horse through. Indians were reported to have burned off large areas of it to make travel easier and to provide more browse for deer. But the oak also served the Indians, for they harvested the acorns and—after grinding, baking, and washing them to remove the inherent bitterness—used them in soups and breads. These extensive stands of Gambel oak serve an important biological purpose by providing cover for certain small animals and birds, and their decaying leaves make the soil rich in nutrients, as shown by the frequency of lupine, geranium, mule ears, and other wild flowers here.

Within a few miles of the top of McClure Pass (only 9,500 feet in elevation) you enter the aspen zone, which provides another of those autumn spectaculars. Practically the entire mountainside south of the pass is covered by an aspen forest. The transition from scrub oak to aspen marks a difference in precipitation, for though it is low by Colorado standards, the McClure Pass area receives more snow, and retains it longer, than the valleys and hillsides below it.

The descent from here into the Crystal River Valley can be a total riot of color in autumn because of both the foliage and the red sandstone cliffs on the opposite side of the valley. Highway 133 follows the Crystal River north to Redstone and Carbondale, a section covered separately because of the side trip to Marble.

FACING PAGE:
The Crystal River

*Marcellina
Mountain*

KEBLER AND OHIO PASSES

THIS IS another tour that begins on Colorado Highway 133, but beyond Paonia and just before you reach Paonia Reservoir, you turn right on an unnumbered road leading into the Gunnison National Forest. The road runs along Anthracite Creek for a short distance, then climbs slowly up out of the valley. To the left is 11,348-foot-high Marcellina Mountain, its flanks creased by erosion to give it an awesomely rugged appearance. Soon you leave the cottonwoods far behind and climb into aspen and spruce forests. To the southwest are the West Elk Mountains, located in the West Elk National Wilderness.

To me this trip is rather special because I discovered one of those delightful jewels of Colorado's High Country—Lost Lake. About ten miles southeast of Highway 133, I followed the US Forest Service signs and turned right on the dirt road. The last mile to the lake is a bit rough and rutted, but by taking it slowly almost any vehicle can make it.

The setting is superb: stately old forests of spruce and fir; tranquil lake with excellent fishing; rugged mountain peak rising above. You'll find wild flowers in profusion here in August: Indian paintbrush, pentstemon, scarlet gilia, and of course the state flower, columbine. The campground at the lake is small and well used despite its relative seclusion. On weekends you may find it filled to capacity, but there are a few places along the road leading here where you can pull into a forest clearing to camp. (Be extra cautious about fires, and be sure to leave the campsite spotlessly clean.)

As Colorado mountain passes go, Kebler, at about 10,000 feet in elevation, is relatively low. You don't quite get up to timberline, but there are beautiful parklike meadows that invite hiking or picnicking. Just beyond Kebler Pass where a spur road leads to Crested Butte, take a sharp right and follow the signs to Ohio Pass, a mere 33 feet higher than Kebler. This is basically the old stage road that used to carry passengers from the train depot in Gunnison to such nearby mining towns as Irwin. In 1882 Irwin was a sizable community that boasted two full-time marshals, several hotels, and 23 saloons and was visited by such notables as General Ulysses S. Grant, Theodore Roosevelt, and Wild Bill Hickok. Within a few years Irwin became a ghost town and its remains can now be visited off the Kebler Pass-Crested Butte spur road by following the Forest Service signs.

Descending the south side of Ohio Pass, the road switchbacks through extensive aspen forests, making it a spectacular trip in the fall. Most people don't realize that aspen forests grow in such dense stands because they spread principally by shoots from the root system. Sometimes an entire grove can originate from a single tree. Furthermore, aspen are frequently a transitory species in forest evolution, beginning their extensive growth on open or sometimes burned-over areas. Douglas fir and Engelmann spruce are often found growing in stands of aspen because the seedlings of these species require shade—provided by the aspen—for the first decade or two of their lives. Eventually the conifers crowd out the aspen and become the climax forest.

Only a few miles from the top of Ohio Pass is a thin, silvery streak of a waterfall that tumbles a hundred feet or more over a cliff above the right side of the road. There's room to pull off here, and a well-beaten trail leads to the base of the falls. Farther on is the valley of Ohio Creek—broad, open ranch country offering distant views of the jagged West Elk Peak. This road takes you past the remnants of several coal mines and ultimately into Gunnison.

REDSTONE AND MARBLE

COLORADO Highway 133 begins and the Crystal River ends just north of Carbondale. Take the highway here south along the river toward Redstone, situated right across from a long line of old coke ovens. Redstone is a picturesque town with high trees shadowing little Victorian houses, the scene dominated by the tall clock tower of the Dutch-style Redstone Inn. The inn stands at the foot of an aspen- and pine-covered slope.

Today Redstone is a resort, but it was founded, in 1902, as a company town, laid out for the miners who worked the local coal mines. John C. Osgood, head of the Colorado Fuel and Iron Company, was shocked by the dilapidated lice-infested shacks and the tents his employees lived in. He planned and built a model village for the workers—about 70 small houses, different in style and color, as well as a large schoolhouse, a clubhouse, and a firehouse. The inn in those days was the bachelor quarters. Only a few of the original houses are still standing, but many of the newer ones are also Victorian in style.

Of course, Osgood didn't exactly neglect himself. About one mile from Redstone he built a 2½-million-dollar Tudor-style manor, which he called Cleveholm. You pass it as you drive down Highway 133.

BELOW: *Redstone Inn*

FACING PAGE: *The West Elk National Wilderness*

For many years I've wondered about the huge marble blocks seen lying in and along the Crystal River. I know they came from the town of (what else?) Marble, but no one has been able to give me an explanation of why so many can be found so far down the river. A flood? Train accidents?

Marble is now a semi-ghost town, reached by turning left on a gravel road south of Placita and following the Crystal River east for a few miles. Although claims had been staked many years before, there was no great demand for marble until a turn-of-the-century fire in New Jersey showed that it could withstand great heat and was good for fireproofing buildings. The business boomed, and the town of Marble came into its own. The crowning achievement of the local mine was quarrying the biggest single piece of marble ever cut; it weighed roughly 100 tons. By the time it became the Tomb of the Unknown Soldier in Washington, D.C., the huge block had been sculpted down to a little more than 60 tons. When marble buildings went out of style, the town died. Two mudslides that wiped out many of the buildings didn't help. Today only a few people live here, most of them in the summer.

The cemetery, a short way out of town, naturally has many marble tombstones. On the grave of one young woman, next to the marble stone giving the necessary information, there is a lovely hand-carved wooden plaque with just KAREN on it. Someone loved her a lot.

Marble piles along the Crystal River

HAGERMAN PASS

CURIOUSLY enough, the 1926 *Rand McNally Auto Road Atlas* shows the Hagerman Pass route as a state highway. Today the old highway is a backroad, but be forewarned that if your car has a low road-clearance, this should be considered a marginal trip—particularly the section at the top of the pass. However, with a moderate amount of clearance or a large amount of luck, the few rough spots can be negotiated. It is well worth the effort, for this is among the most scenically spectacular trips in Colorado, with some fascinating railroad history to boot.

You can start the trip on US Highway 24 just south of Leadville, one of the most famous mining towns on the Western fron-

tier. If you're heading south, take the first road to the right, and follow signs to Turquoise Lake. West of the lake you'll climb steadily up an old railbed blasted out of the side of a large, forested canyon. At the head of the gorge, where the road curves to follow the north slope, is the Carlton Tunnel. Today it sits in disrepair with NO TRESPASSING signs plastered on the rusting iron gate that blocks its entrance. At one time, however, the tunnel represented a marvelous feat in railroad engineering.

When the Colorado Midland Railway Company constructed its line from Leadville to Aspen Junction (now Basalt), it had to contend with a formidable barrier, the Sawatch

BELOW: *Turquoise
Lake with
Mount Elbert in
the distance*

FACING PAGE:
Lost Lake

Range. Some of Colorado's most rugged peaks are in this mountain chain, including Mount Elbert, the highest point in the state, with an elevation of 14,433 feet. The railroad followed the most gradual slope up toward Hagerman Pass, but the company opted to build a tunnel at the 11,528-foot level to alleviate the need for a steep, tough grade over the top. The 2,164-foot-long Hagerman Tunnel, completed in 1888, was not entirely sat-

isfactory. Heavy snows on a steeper-than-normal grade posed problems for the trains. So in 1890 an independent company that was hoping to profit from tolls blasted the Busk-Ivanhoe Tunnel (now called the Carlton) through almost two miles of solid granite at an elevation almost 600 feet lower than the Hagerman Tunnel. This new shaft eliminated about seven rail miles. Even though the Colorado Midland paid steep

rates to the private company, they were lower than the maintenance costs on the higher route. In 1897, however, new owners of the Colorado Midland sought to save money by reopening the higher and tougher Hagerman Tunnel. The move proved an economic disaster. A bitter winter accompanied by ferocious blizzards closed the line for 78 days, and the company never recovered from the lost revenues in passenger and freight haulage between Aspen and Leadville. Eventually the Busk-Ivanhoe (Carlton) Tunnel was converted to an auto toll road, then abandoned.

Today the Hagerman Tunnel cannot be seen from the present road, but in the vicinity of the Carlton Tunnel an unmarked trail ascends steep hillsides about 600 vertical feet to the old tunnel.

Beyond the Carlton Tunnel the road climbs very steeply in a series of panoramic switchbacks. Near the expansive open top of Hagerman Pass on the Continental Divide, I had to get a running start to cross a small muddy patch of snow, but I made it.

The road down the west side of the pass gets rough in a few places, with a steep incline, ruts, and rocks to slow down the pace. The views are superb. Below is the alpine basin formed by the upper Fryingpan River. All around are high, snow-clad peaks. The road twists gradually downward across flower-dotted tundra and a couple of small streams. In a few miles you enter the Hell Gate area where the old railroad (now the road) was blasted through a precipitous, narrow gorge. In the days when the railroad was in operation, trains used to stop here to allow

LEFT: Cars of the old Colorado Midland Railway at Hell Gate

FACING PAGE: *Coal Creek*

View of mountains from the Hagerman Pass road

passengers the opportunity to disembark and look over the edge into the frightening depths of the canyon. It's still a little disconcerting today to peer out the driver's side and see the rusting hulks of a few vehicles that didn't make it lying mangled on the rocks many hundreds of feet below.

After passing the lovely Ruedi Reservoir, the road enters a canyon of colorful rock formations and eventually emerges at the town of Basalt on Colorado Highway 82, in the Roaring Fork Valley. To the southeast is Aspen, and to the northwest, Glenwood Springs. Despite some tough driving, this is a dazzling trip with an incredible variety of beautiful scenery.

Colorado Sketch: THE LEADVILLE ICE PALACE

AN ACTIVE mining town is a pretty ugly thing. Leadville in its heyday was no exception. Huge mine dumps, smoke from the many smelters in the valley, and hillsides denuded for fuel left much to be desired in the beauty department. After the repeal of the Sherman Silver Purchase Act in 1893 brought silver mining to an end in the vicinity, reclamation and civic beautification were the last things on Leadville's collective mind. Unemployment and economic disaster were the first things.

So it comes as somewhat of a surprise to learn that in the midst of all this ugliness a structure of great and unusual beauty was built—the Leadville ice palace. It began as a plan for bringing much-needed tourist dollars into the town.

Tourist schemes were not new to the state. Pueblo had its mineral palace in 1890, and every town and city had mini-festivals of one kind or another. Leadville, with its lengthy winters, seemed ideal for a monumental ice structure—its climate has been described as "ten months winter and two months mighty late fall." The same railroad that used to carry silver out of the town could bring in tourists from Denver. Why, it would undoubtedly bring in people from all over the world and each and every one of them would be loaded with money to spend in Leadville.

Work on the palace was started in November 1895, with a target opening date of Christmas. This wasn't a small undertaking—the palace turned out to be the largest ice structure ever built in the United States, maybe in the world. When the people of Leadville dreamed, they dreamed big. The site occupied five acres. The building itself was longer than a football field and almost twice as wide. The architect, who had built a smaller ice palace in St. Paul, Minnesota, designed a Norman-style castle with octagonal, 90-foot-high towers flanking the entrance.

By the first week of December, the wooden interior had been finished and excellent progress was being made on the five-foot-thick outside ice walls. Then the grandiose plans almost went, literally, down the drain. An unheard-of midwinter thaw brought 50- to 60-degree daytime temperatures for almost three weeks. About the only things that saved the structure were the below-freezing nighttime temperatures and 10,000 yards of canvas draped over the ice during the day. When the thaw broke just before Christmas and the temperature went back to its customary frigid state, construction was behind schedule. On December 30, the workmen broke all their previous records, but there was still some work to be finished when the Leadville ice palace was opened with much fanfare on January 1, 1896. The town's merchants had given their clerks a half day off, and the miners had been given a day off (without pay, of course) to attend the parade and opening speeches. All of Leadville lined up to pay the 50-cent admission fee.

And what of all those hordes of expected Denverites and world citizens who would spend mightily to see such a wonder? Well, they came, all right, clutching sack lunches, but not in droves. They saw the amazing structure with its 16,000-square-foot skating rink and two ballrooms, looked over the exhibits frozen in the inside walls, and left on the afternoon train. The whole endeavor was a financial bust.

By mid-February, Leadville was sick of ice-skating and tobogganing and rock-drilling contests. The weather turned unseasonably warm the first of March and stayed warm. There was nothing to do but close the palace down. The official ceremonies putting an end to the venture were held on March 28.

It had been a grand idea, beautifully executed. Nature and the Denverites just hadn't cooperated.

55

*The Leadville
Ice Palace*

*Storm clouds
over Weston Pass*

WESTON PASS

THIS ROAD follows the old stage route from the broad, mountain-rimmed valley called South Park to the upper Arkansas Valley near Leadville. In 1879 the Denver, South Park and Pacific Railway was extended south several miles past Fairplay to the short-lived town of Weston. There, supplies were unloaded and passengers disembarked for the rough trip to Leadville by way of 11,900-foot-high Weston Pass. The stage lines did a brisk business, one of them grossing nearly half a million dollars in that one year alone, ferrying passengers and freight from the railhead to California Gulch, site of mining activity in the Leadville region. By 1880, when the Denver and Rio Grande Western Railroad was extended into the Arkansas Valley and up to Leadville, stage and freight traffic over Weston Pass diminished radically.

The route today can be easily reached by turning west off US Highway 285 about ten miles south of Fairplay (some signs are posted). The first part of the road traverses the western edge of South Park and climbs gradually. The last few miles to the top of the pass are steep and rocky. Depending on rain and snow conditions, you may find this section of the road seriously rutted, making it difficult, if not impossible, to drive on.

When I was only a mile or so from the top, I stopped to photograph the wild flowers. The open meadows here were lush green, and near a spring I found beautiful blue columbines growing in profusion—a rather unusual phenomenon, or so I thought, for most columbines seem to prefer the shade of forests.

At the top of the pass there are the remains of some old structures, perhaps part of a mining operation or, more likely, a way station for the stage lines. The only building to survive intact is a lonely old outhouse.

Starting down the west side of the pass, the road becomes rough and rutted again, but gradually it smooths out and winds down into a wooded canyon where it follows a stream. Beavers have been at work here. The dams they've built have created terraces of ponds over nearly a half mile stretch. Aspen, a favored food of beavers (they eat the succulent inner bark as well as the leaves and shoots), has been cut and dragged a long distance to serve as building materials for these mammalian engineers.

After almost giving up hope of finding a suitable camping spot, I found an idyllic place in a small meadow next to the stream. By climbing a hillside nearby, I was rewarded with a superb view of Mount Elbert and the Sawatch Range. It was near sunset, and the breakup of a storm over the distant mountains produced an incredible play of light, shadow, and color on Colorado's highest peak.

The next morning I emerged from this steep little canyon, drove over rolling hills in the Arkansas Valley, and came to US Highway 24. To the left is Buena Vista, and about nine miles to the right is Leadville.

COMO TO BOREAS PASS AND BRECKENRIDGE

BOREAS PASS on the Continental Divide used to be one of the most feared mountain passes in Colorado. Swept by ferocious winds and storms (Boreas was the Greek god of the north wind), the road up to the 11,482-foot-high pass climbed steeply in sharp switchbacks, seeming to cling "to the edge of eternity," as a frontier poet put it.

In spite of the dangers involved, the Boreas Pass road was a major stage route leading from Como in South Park to Breckenridge. Later, the narrow-gauge Denver, South Park and Pacific Railway was extended over the pass, becoming, for a time, the highest railroad in the country. There's a story told about the Barnum Circus train getting stuck here three miles from the top. Common sense ruled—the elephants were let out of their cars and made to push the train the rest of the way.

Today Boreas Pass is reached by turning north off US Highway 285 midway between Jefferson and Fairplay. In less than a mile you come to the almost deserted town of Como, marked by the large stone ruins of a railroad roundhouse. Como was a railroad town named after Italy's Lake Como by homesick Italian coal miners who worked the mines nearby. When it was first founded it was built entirely of tents, the better to pick up and move to Leadville when the railroad construction crews moved on. When the trains no longer came through South Park, the town's population dwindled to the few people it now has.

A dirt road northwest of town follows the old Denver, South Park and Pacific roadbed to the pass. Within the last 20 years the Army Corps of Engineers stationed at Fort Carson dredged the railroad route and

59

converted it for automobiles. There's a marker along the way in memory of a soldier who was killed while on duty here.

As you ascend the pass, you'll notice signs of mining activity everywhere—a large tramway, a tall loading device, many buildings. On the summit is an old log section house left over from the days of the railroad.

On your way down the other side of the Divide, you'll come to Baker's Tank, a way station which supplied the trains with water from 1882 to 1937. Baker's Tank has been preserved by the US Forest Service. The deforested hillsides serve as another reminder of the railroads and the mining operations in the area.

The road continues on to Breckenridge, now a popular ski resort. It started out as a mining camp, and was named after US Vice-President John C. Breckinridge, in the hopes of getting a post office through his political influence. It worked. A couple of years later, the townspeople were incensed to learn that Breckinridge's sympathies lay with the Confederate States, so they changed the town name to BreckENridge. (That'll show him!) By the way, if you're in Breckenridge at the right time of the year, you can say you've been out of the United States. Three days out of every August the town is declared a "no man's land." It seems that the area was overlooked in the official steps that led to Colorado's becoming a state in 1876, and when the city fathers of Breckenridge finally "consented" to join the Union—which they did in 1936—the town reserved the right to be a "free and independent kingdom for three days each year."

RIGHT: *Log building with stained-glass window in Como*

FACING PAGE: *Abandoned mining tram near Boreas Pass*

Horses and cattle
near Hoosier Pass

ALMA AND FAIRPLAY

SOUTH of Breckenridge, Colorado Highway 9 crosses the Continental Divide over Hoosier Pass (elevation 11,541 feet). South of the pass, at its foot, lies the town of Alma. It was in this vicinity that the legend of Silver Heels sprang up.

Silver Heels was the name the miners gave to the beautiful dance hall girl who came to the area about 1861. When tragedy struck in the form of a smallpox epidemic, a frantic message was sent to Denver for help, but few persons were willing to come or able to nurse the dying miners. Silver Heels went from cabin to cabin helping in any way she could—bringing food here, comforting a sick man there. Then she too came down with the horrible disease. Gradually, the sickness waned, and the grateful miners raised some 5,000 dollars to present to their heroine. She

was nowhere to be found. Did she disappear because she was terribly scarred? Did she go off somewhere to die? Mount Silverheels behind Fairplay is named in her honor.

The little cemetery in Alma, where many of the smallpox victims were buried, can be reached by taking Park County 8 opposite the Alma post office. Follow this route to the Buckskin Cemetery sign, then double back on the dirt road to the right.

It's a lovely place, set in a grove of aspen and evergreens. Wild flowers grow in between and on top of the graves. Many of them have iron or wooden fences around them (to keep out the wild animals—a chilling thought). The whole history of the area can be read on the tombstones—many babies who didn't make it to their first birthdays, whole families dead in some epidemic, a mother and her newborn baby buried together, a man who went out to visit his mine in a snowstorm and wasn't found until June. Death was a real part of these people's lives. Maybe because of that there's a feeling about this cemetery of caring—of wanting the dead to have a beautiful, natural setting in which to spend eternity—that is lacking in modern, well-manicured memorial parks.

Highway 9 follows the South Platte River from Alma to Fairplay. Along the way you'll notice large dredging piles, where the riverbed was scooped up, sifted for gold, and then dumped. In this environmentally conscious age it's hard to conceive of dredging operations being not just tolerated but actually encouraged. It's understandable, however, when you realize that any kind of mining operation meant a town would live and not fade away as so many others had. It didn't matter that the ugly, scarring dredging was at the very edge of the town itself.

Fairplay didn't fade away, obviously, and today is the county seat of Park County.

Incidentally, when the town was nothing but a group of log cabins, one of the prospectors declared himself the boss and proclaimed "fairplay" for everyone. This early politician later became a notorious highwayman. Times haven't changed much.

Fairplay has done a good job of preserving its history. There are many reconstructed old houses—from log cabins to ornate Victorian buildings—in the South Park City Museum, a restored pioneer village on the outskirts of town. Many of the buildings were moved here from nearby ghost towns but some are on their original sites.

On Fairplay's main street, you'll notice a most unusual monument. This was erected by the townspeople over the grave of one of their premier "citizens" (described next), the inspiration for a yearly race that draws spectators from miles around.

*Tombstones in
Buckskin Cemetery
near Alma*

*Chapel in
South Park Village*

Colorado Sketch: PRUNES, A BURRO

THEY COULD be stubborn, they weren't very sweet smelling, and they were certainly loud. The first Colorado miner to call burros "Rocky Mountain Canaries" had probably spent many a sleepless night listening to the harsh high-pitched braying of his four-legged companion. But when gold was discovered in the state, the burro turned out to be the perfect beast of burden for the prospectors who began tramping all over the High Country in search of the yellow metal.

Strong and reliable, this small donkey was the ideal pack animal. He could carry his owner, he could carry his owner's mining tools and personal gear, and if his owner were lucky enough to find it, he could carry out the gold.

The burro's surefootedness was indispensable on steep mountain slopes. He could go for long periods of time without food or water in emergencies, but if there were water to be found, his keen nose would sniff it out. He had an uncanny knack of getting himself—and his owner—out of tight predicaments. No wonder a prospector valued a good burro.

Prunes was more than a good burro. Prunes was one of the best.

Rupert M. Sherwood needed a burro, now that he was going into the prospecting business full time. He'd heard that a miner who was retiring had an experienced "canary" for sale. The burro had worked the mines in Alma and Fairplay. Twelve years old, in the prime of life. Ten bucks the owner wanted for him.

Rupe looked the little brown animal over thoroughly. The burro seemed strong and healthy enough, his teeth were good, he seemed bright and alert.

"You can't go wrong," the owner said.

"What's his name?" Rupe asked as he handed over the ten dollars.

"Prunes," was the answer.

Rupe eyed the burro's shaggy form. "It figures," he said.

Rupe and Prunes were well-suited to each other, and a strong bond developed between man and animal. The two of them were soon functioning as partners.

The burro's role went beyond that of the typical pack animal. The ever-dependable Prunes could be trusted to run errands by himself. He would find his way down the trail and into a town, mosey over to the general store, wait for the written order he carried to be filled and the supplies loaded on his back, then tote them up to their camp.

Rupe and Prunes worked all over the Alma and Fairplay areas, sometimes prospecting on their own, sometimes hiring out to one of the big mining companies.

Rupe never did get rich, but he made enough to take care of the two of them and even managed to put aside something for his old age.

Old age did come—to both of them. As the years went by Rupe's aching bones bothered him more and more, but not from the hard work of prospecting—that just loosened him up, made him feel alive. No, it was those windy Fairplay winters he couldn't stand. The city comforts and warmth of Denver began to look pretty tempting to the prospector.

But what about Prunes? There was no way Rupe could take him to Denver for the winter, and he couldn't bear to sell his companion of almost 50 years. Why, it would be like selling his own brother. But Prunes was too old to be just turned out to fend for himself. Still, that appeared to be the only answer to the problem.

Rupe soon found that he didn't have to worry about Prunes's well-being. The inhabitants of Fairplay considered him to be something of a town institution and took over the responsibility of feeding him during the long winters.

Rupe returned to Fairplay in the summers, and he and Prunes would spend the few warm months together. Then Rupe would go to Denver when the weather turned cold and Prunes would once again resume his daily treks up and down the streets of Fairplay, stopping at each house to get a handout.

Prunes was 63 when he died in 1930. He was buried on Front Street, in the heart of Fairplay. Beside his grave the townspeople erected a monument of stone and concrete. But this wasn't your everyday monument—that wouldn't have done justice to the faithful Prunes.

His tombstone is surmounted by a bronze plaque, with the image of the little burro in bas-relief. At the sides are display cases holding newspaper articles about him and his master. The entire monument is decorated with samples of ore from all the mines that Prunes once served. The inscription reads: "Prunes. A Burro. 1867-1930. Fairplay. Alma. All mines in this district." Originally this was spelled out in colored marbles.

Rupe Sherwood died the next year, at the age of 81. In accordance with his last wish, his ashes were buried at the base of Prunes's monument. An iron fence, ornamented with Rupe's mining tools, surrounds the two graves. Rupe and Prunes just hated to be apart.

The townspeople of Fairplay haven't forgotten Prunes and the other "canaries" that worked the mines in the area. Every year, on the last full weekend of July, they stage the 23-mile World's Championship Pack Burro Race along a course over Mosquito Pass. An eye-catching bumper sticker—"Get Your Ass up the Pass"—helps advertise the event. The burros are fitted with regulation pack saddles, loaded with 25-pound weights, and decorated with old-time gold mining equipment. Then they are pulled or cajoled over the 13,188-foot-high pass. The owners are not allowed to ride or prod the burros but may carry them (none has done this so far) or tug at them with a 15-foot-long lead rope. To date, the record time for the round-trip event is two hours, 50 minutes, and 46½ seconds. A parade, dance, barbecue, melodrama, and turkey shoot are part of the weekend festivities.

8 mi.

N

FAIRPLAY

GARO

US 285

HARTSEL

ANTERO JCT.

SOUTH PARK

South Platte River

TARRYALL MTS.

FLORISSANT

Florissant Fossil Beds Nat'l Mon.

US 24

MANITOU SPRS.

+ Pikes Peak

COLORADO SPRINGS

CRIPPLE CREEK

VICTOR

+ Little Pisgah Peak

Cripple Cr.

Fourmile Cr.

Phantom Canyon

9

To Gunnison

SALIDA

PONCHA SPRINGS

Arkansas River

Access road to Royal Gorge

Royal Gorge

CANON CITY

I 25

US 50

PUEBLO

THE ROYAL GORGE TO SOUTH PARK

A TOUR of the Royal Gorge—the incredible canyon carved by the Arkansas River—hardly qualifies as a backroad trip because of its proximity to US Highway 50, a heavily traveled route from Pueblo to Salida, Gunnison, and points west. Nonetheless, this 1,000-foot-deep defile (in places only 30 feet wide) is a popular tourist attraction and you will undoubtedly want to visit it if you are in the area. About eight miles west of Canon City on US 50 is the access road to the gorge.

A mile or so west of the Royal Gorge turnoff on US 50 begins Colorado Highway 9. Although it does not have the most beautiful mountain scenery in Colorado, this route

BELOW: *Hills along
Colorado Highway 9
near Hartsel*

FACING PAGE:
*Glacier Gorge
in Rocky Mountain
National Park*

is a very pleasant and somewhat different approach to Colorado's mountain-rimmed jewel, South Park. Turning right (northwest) onto Highway 9, you wind between low piñon- and juniper-covered hills for several miles and climb gradually in elevation. So subtle is the gradient that you only become aware of the change in elevation by noting that the piñon and juniper community is replaced by open, grass-covered hillsides. Ranches dot these hills, and white-faced Herefords graze along the road. The total gain in altitude from US 50 to Fairplay in the northwest corner of South Park is approximately 4,000 feet.

After passing through a small segment of the Pike National Forest you enter the valley called South Park. This high, broad, grassy basin (it's roughly 40 miles long by 30 wide) was first visited as early as 1803 by a Kentucky trapper, James Purcell, who claimed to have found gold here. In 1806 the Zebulon Pike expedition entered the valley over a route paralleling Highway 9 from the vicinity of the Royal Gorge. For the next two decades the valley was visited by occasional fur trappers in search of beaver. John Charles Frémont reported finding large herds of buffalo and other game (presumably elk and deer) in South Park when he traversed it on his way to California in 1844. This area, in fact, was long a traditional hunting ground for the Utes, and even certain Plains Indians migrated here seasonally for the hunt. Traditionally, much of the buffalo meat was cut into strips and "jerked," or cured by drying in the sun. Pemmican—basically a mixture of powdered dried meat and fat with berries and other ingredients sometimes added—was a valuable and nutritious food for the

Indians when traveling in regions where game was sparse. The mountain men, or fur trappers of the time, adopted it as an important food source during their far-ranging journeys.

In the years following Colorado's first gold discoveries, South Park was an important route to the various strikes. The area itself had some significant deposits of the yellow metal along the South Platte River near Fairplay and Alma and in the Tarryall region north of the valley. In 1879, when the Denver, South Park and Pacific Railway entered South Park from the northeast, the valley became a shipping and transportation center, serving the various mining districts to the west.

South Park is one of those special places in Colorado. The valley today has numerous large ranches. In my travels I've found few places to match it for scenic beauty. As a photographer I especially appreciate the interplay here of storms, clouds, lighting, mountains, and soft, lovely land. There seems to be a never-ending variety of photographic possibilities. I once chased a rainbow for several miles between Fairplay and Red Hill Pass, finally capturing it on film as it arched above a small farm. Sunsets and sunrises here seem to have a special quality and intensity of color.

The road continues to Hartsel, where it crosses US Highway 24, then passes through Garo (once a way station for the Denver, South Park and Pacific line), and ends near Fairplay at US Highway 285. These last few miles along the South Platte River from Hartsel to Fairplay give you another glimpse of the unpleasant aspects of gold mining. An abandoned dredge sits in the river channel amid spoil piles of boulders and gravel. It seems likely that this segment of the South Platte will not recover from the damage for a very long time.

LEFT: *Rainbow over South Park*

FACING PAGE: *Blue spruce and aspen in the San Juan Mountains*

71

FLORISSANT AND CRIPPLE CREEK

SOUTHWEST of Pikes Peak, along a rocky little stream known as Cripple Creek, lies one of the most famous goldfields in the world—the Cripple Creek Gold District. A worthless-looking six-square-mile plateau in the crater of an extinct volcano, it has yielded more than 430 million dollars in the precious metal since the 1890s—more than any other single gold deposit ever found. At one time, however, no one would believe there was gold here.

Compared to other gold strikes in Colorado, the Cripple Creek boom started late. The discovery of gold was delayed by a hoax. It all started in 1884 when two prospectors, apparently at the urging of some business-hungry merchants of Canon City, "salted" a vein of rock in the Cripple Creek area. This rock with its falsely loaded gold assayed at a fabulously rich 2,000 dollars per ton, and news of its discovery immediately precipitated a rush to what was called the

Mount Pisgah Gold Field (named for the prominent volcanic peak nearby). After a month of feverish digging, the hoax became apparent, and the thousands who had flocked here left in disgust. The incident left a tainted image of the area in the minds of other prospectors, and for the next half-dozen years few bothered to check into the possibility of real gold in the region.

When a local rancher and cowpoke, Bob Womack, made the first discovery of gold, he had a credibility problem. Besides the bad image left by the Mount Pisgah hoax,

Womack—dubbed "Crazy Bob" locally—had a reputation for being unstable and unreliable. Thus, little credence was given his 1890 strike at first, even after assays showed the ore to be worth 250 dollars per ton—a moderately good value in those days. Gradually, however, the word of gold spread, and by 1891 the boom was on. Like many other prospectors of the time, Womack died broke, having gotten ripsnorting drunk and sold his claim for 500 dollars. Over the next several decades the Cripple Creek Gold District produced an estimated 400 million dollars'

*Stage to
old Cripple Creek
mining camp*

*Cripple Creek
in 1897*

worth of the glittering metal and made mil-
lionaires of almost 30 men.

To me the most scenic route leading to
the town of Cripple Creek is through Florissant Fossil Beds National Monument. From
US Highway 24 west of Colorado Springs,
turn off at the town of Florissant (French for
"flowering" or "blooming") and head south.
About a mile from US 24, you enter the
national monument, and about two miles
farther is the Visitor Center.

This area was the subject of a conservation controversy in the 1960s when some fossil beds here were threatened by land
development schemes. In 1969 Congress
established the national monument to preserve these paleontological treasures. A stop
at the Visitor Center is vital if you hope to
understand the significance of the place, for
on display are rare, delicate, and exquisitely
beautiful fossilized remains of insects and
plants that were trapped by spewing volcanic ash and lava flows, 35 million years

ago. The fossils provide valuable scientific
information about life forms in the Oligo-
cene epoch. There are also some petrified
sequoia stumps in the monument, reached
by a short hike from the Visitor Center.

The road climbs gradually as you continue south, then descends into the basin
where Cripple Creek is located. Though it is
backroads country today, Cripple Creek is
definitely not a ghost town. Devastated by a
couple of major fires, the community not
only survived but somehow managed to
retain much of its turn-of-the-century boomtown flavor. It once boasted some 40 assay
offices, 14 newspapers, 70 saloons, and a
notorious red-light district—Myers Avenue.
Two electric trolleys served the area. Like
Central City (described later), the Cripple
Creek region today is a major tourist
attraction.

Mining towns are often associated with
famous people, and Cripple Creek is no
exception. Lowell Thomas spent his early

years here. Jack Johnson, the first black heavyweight champion of the world, was a bouncer in a local saloon, and Jack Dempsey worked in one of the mines.

In visiting Cripple Creek, allow enough time to simply wander around town and absorb some of its flavor and character. You can also take a ride on a restored narrow-gauge railroad or collect mineral specimens from the numerous mine tailings throughout the area.

Continuing south, the road leads to Victor, another boomtown, which had several famous gold mines nearby, then descends steeply through Phantom Canyon, a magnificent gorge, and follows one of the old railroad routes. The steep, heavily forested walls of the canyon rise high above, making this a breathtaking trip. Eventually the road emerges from the gorge and travels across dry, open land to intersect US Highway 50 east of Canon City.

*The road from
Cripple Creek to
US Highway 50*

*The Pikes Peak
road before the days
of the automobile*

Colorado Sketch: THE PIKES PEAK HILL CLIMB

IT WAS 1916. Americans were enthralled with Mary Pickford, embroiled in a presidential election, and reading Booth Tarkington's best-seller *Seventeen*. They were also in love with the automobile. Thanks to Henry Ford and his 320-dollar tin lizzie, almost 4 million Americans now owned a car. It was no longer a rich man's toy.

The popularity of the automobile hadn't escaped the notice of Spencer Penrose of Colorado Springs. Always one to keep an eye open for any profitable enterprise, he had already begun to formulate plans for a surefire money-maker. "Why not," he postulated, "build a toll road up Pikes Peak?" So what if there was already a cog railroad going to the top? Tourists would be willing to shell out plenty for the privilege of driving their own cars to the summit.

He applied to the Department of Agriculture for a permit and franchise. "Might be pretty expensive," he was told. "The road might cost you as much as 25,000 dollars."

"That's no problem, I've got the money," he said. "Shouldn't be too hard. We'll just follow the old carriage road."

One year and 250,000 dollars later, the road to the summit of Pikes Peak was finished.

"Well," said Penrose, "it cost a bit more than I thought, and we still have to compete with the cog railroad. Guess we'd better do a little advertising to start the money rolling in."

Penrose was never one to do anything halfway. His idea of a "little advertising" was to organize one of the most spectacular auto races of the decade—the Pikes Peak Hill Climb.

The Pikes Peak auto race captured the imagination of the country. Driving to the summit was one thing. Two cars had already done that, long before the road was built—a locomobile in 1901 and a Buick Bearcat in 1913. But racing to the top—when a wrong move could mean plunging over the side of the mountain into some deep abyss—now *that* was exciting. It was better than the Indianapolis 500.

Penrose made sure the public's interest remained high by signing up Barney Oldfield, the first man to go a mile a minute on an oval track, as a contestant. If anybody could bring in the crowds, it would be this auto-racing hero.

The hill climb was actually several races, run over two days. The cars were classified according to weight and piston displacement. The thousands of spectators who lined the road that first day, August 11, 1916, were there not only for the races, but also for the chance to view the most magnificent sports cars of the day. In addition to the Lexingtons, Packards, Dodges, Stutzes, Hudsons, and Chevrolets, there were a Rolls Royce and a Duesenberg entered. Oldfield was driving a 30,000-dollar French Delage and was quite obviously the crowd's favorite.

Then they were off in a cloud of dust—literally. Around those hairpin curves, skidding on the steep grades, the cars raced the 12 miles to the finish line. And when the first day's racing was over, the winner and champion was—Fred Junk in a Chalmers. And when the second day's racing was over, the winner was—Ray Lentz in a Romano. Barney Oldfield did no better than twelfth. The altitude had affected his car.

In spite of the embarrassing defeat of its favorite, the crowd proclaimed the Pikes Peak Hill Climb a huge success, and it became an annual event. Today the auto race from Manitou Springs to the summit and back is held on a July Sunday every year, and a footrace along the same route is staged every summer.

As for the road, it too was a success, although it wasn't as profitable as Penrose would have wished. It turned out to be very expensive to maintain. When Penrose's franchise ran out in 1936, he shed no tears. For one thing, he was much too busy running the Pikes Peak Cog Railway, which he'd bought when he saw how financially successful it could become. (The train *still* makes several trips a day out of Manitou Springs in the summer.) Spencer Penrose always did know how to turn a tidy profit.

THE FRONT AND RAMPART RANGES

THERE ARE numerous roads, old and new, penetrating the Front Range area between Denver and Colorado Springs. Each of them is somewhat different in its history and scenery. Because of their proximity to the heavily populated areas of Denver and Colorado Springs, the Front Range—the easternmost extension of the Rockies—and the Rampart Range—its southern extension—are more extensively visited than other parts of Colorado. Nevertheless, there are many out-of-the-way places of interest in the region, and you can spend several days exploring them. But be sure to follow the map of this tour, or you may find yourself lost at times in the maze of roads.

One short trip begins in Morrison, west of Denver, where Colorado Highway 8 runs into Colorado 74, which climbs through the lovely, twisting canyon formed by Bear Creek and ends in Evergreen. Less well known is the route that leads southeast from

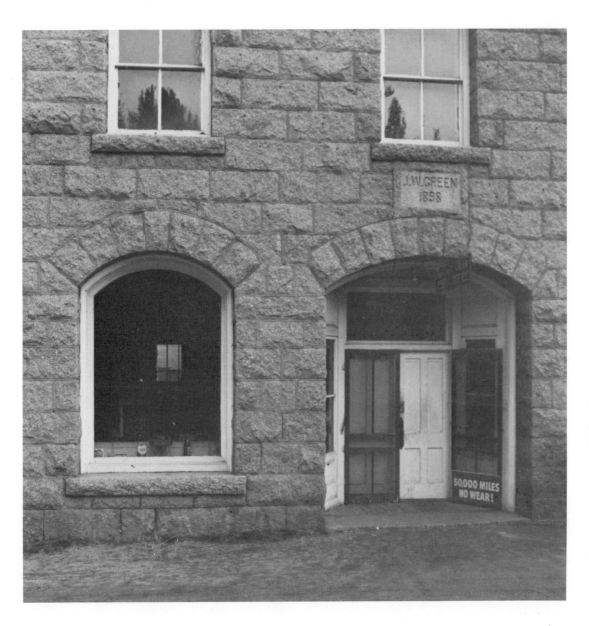

*The Green
Mercantile store
in Buffalo Creek*

79

US Highway 285 at Pine Junction, located just southwest of Conifer. The road descends to the little town of Pine, but before you get there you may want to take the turnoff to Pine Valley Ranch. This restored old log ranch, tucked way off the road in isolation, offers some of the finest gourmet cuisine in the Denver area. Turning left in Pine, which is on the North Fork of the South Platte River, you can follow a narrow, twisting road through the village of Sphinx Park, nestled among smoothly polished granite walls and great monoliths that rise abruptly from the deep canyon. Continuing on the main road a few miles past Pine, you come to the town of Buffalo Creek. If time allows, you should visit the Green Mercantile, a genuine old country store—the very antithesis of a modern supermarket—housed in a massive granite-block building northwest of town. It has been run by three generations of the same family since 1883. Buffalo Creek, incidentally, lies along the route of the old Denver, South Park and Pacific Railway. In fact, just behind the Green Mercantile is part of the old railbed.

At Buffalo Creek, you have several options. You can turn left and follow the road to Foxton, gradually climbing up Kennedy Gulch to join US 285 again just south of Conifer. Or you can follow the road to the right, which climbs hills and dips into forested valleys, then loops to the northwest to emerge at US 285 in the town of Bailey. Your third choice is to drive straight ahead about 15 miles to the town of Deckers, situated on the main branch of the South Platte River. There are spectacular views along this stretch: jagged granite peaks, the plains beyond, thickly forested canyons. There are

also many US Forest Service campgrounds and picnic areas to choose from. Deckers was once a popular vacation spot for wealthy Denver families in the days before autos and interstates and ski resorts. The setting here is pleasant indeed.

The road intersects Colorado Highway 67 at Deckers. To the left the highway follows the South Platte River for a short distance, then continuing northeast climbs steeply out of the canyon and descends to the town of Sedalia on US Highway 85, in the plains. About 14 miles northeast of Deckers, halfway to Sedalia, you have still another fascinating option, a side trip down the Rampart Range Road. Well-marked, this road heads south for almost 40 miles before joining US Highway 24 at Woodland Park, northwest of Colorado Springs. Along the way be sure to stop at the Devils Head parking area and take the short hike to the Devils Head fire lookout tower, where there are superb views of Denver and the plains. Devils Head is another of those places purported to have buried treasure. Here, according to local legend, is 60,000 dollars in gold eagles, the loot from a robbery of a government train in the 1870s. Before they were captured, the robbers buried the money and marked the spot with a knife in a nearby tree. As in most treasure tales, the men never returned to retrieve the gold (some versions of this story allege that they were killed shortly after burying it) and it's still there for the finding.

If you choose to follow Highway 67 to the southeast at Deckers, it will take you through rolling, forested countryside past many farms and ranches. This road too joins US 24 at Woodland Park.

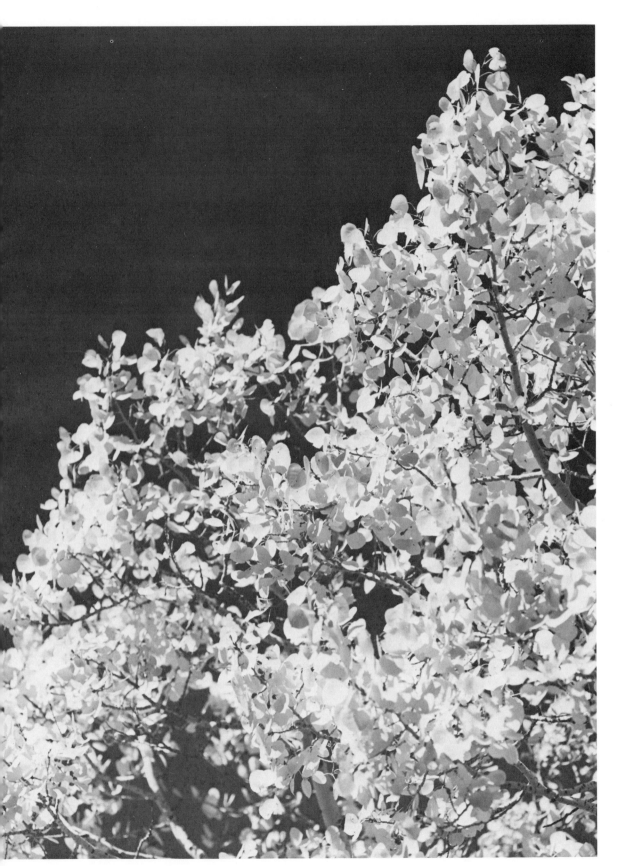

Autumn aspen

Colorado Sketch: THE DINOSAUR HUNTERS

A FEW MILES west of Denver, the first foothills of the Rockies rise abruptly from the flat plains in a long ridge known locally as the Hogback. This area is a favorite spot for school field trips because of the abundance of fossils.

I was along with my son's class one day when suddenly a little boy yelled, "I found one! I found one! I found a dinosaur!"

Well, not quite. The small gray rock he held out so proudly for everyone to admire contained the fossilized remains of some long-dead plant.

But it easily could have been a dinosaur fragment. A bone found in almost this same spot 100 years ago touched off an era of dinosaur discoveries that unearthed most of the species of these prehistoric creatures we know today.

Dinosaurs, generally, were enormous reptiles with small brains. They lived for 130 million years, then mysteriously died out. When an individual dinosaur died and was covered with sand, gradually silica or other mineral compounds replaced the bone and the animal turned to stone—became fossilized. The largest of these monsters lived in the Jurassic age, so the rock laid down during this age, the Morrison formation, yields the fossils of these super-dinosaurs.

Now, nobody knew all this in 1877, least of all schoolteacher Arthur Lakes. All he knew was that he had found a mighty big vertebra near the town of Morrison, Colorado, while out hunting fossilized leaves. He sent a description of it to paleontologist Othniel Marsh. Marsh's ho-hum reply was that he'd have to see it to identify it. Lakes went back to the Hogback and, sure enough, found more bones. This time he sent specimens not only to Marsh, but also to another well-known paleontologist, Edmond Cope.

What Lakes didn't realize was that these two eminent scientists were bitter personal and professional enemies, jealous of each other's accomplishments. When they found that the bones they now held belonged to a prehistoric monster 50 to 60 feet long—the largest yet discovered—the scientific fireworks were set off.

Since Marsh had sent Lakes 100 dollars for the specimens, he could claim the Morrison site. Cope had to relinquish his fossils to Marsh.

The Morrison formation, however, is extensive. Another schoolteacher, O. W. Lucas, was puttering around in the Morrison near Canon City, Colorado, when he too found some enormous bone fossils. This time Cope was the beneficiary of the specimens. They turned out to be even larger than the ones Lakes had found. Cope lost no time in getting his men to the Canon City site.

In 1877 there was still another great dinosaur graveyard discovery. Two railroad men sent Marsh word of an area where bones littered the landscape for seven miles around. The fossil deposits at Como Bluff, Wyoming, were every bit as spectacular as they had said, and Marsh worked the Morrison formation there for 12 years. It yielded 26 new species of the Jurassic dinosaurs.

Year after year after year, tons of fossilized bone were dug from these fantastic dinosaur quarries. Both Cope's and Marsh's men worked summer and winter, always wary for spies from the other camp. The game was find 'em, dig 'em out, and publish before the other one could. Unfortunately, Cope, because of bad financial investments, ran out of money and had to give up the expensive pleasure of dinosaur hunting.

The feud was over. And while most feuds are destructive, this one was not. Two very positive things came out of it.

The obvious gain was the vast amount of knowledge gleaned by the scientific community.

Before Cope and Marsh began their dinosaur hunting, these prehistoric animals were known only from bits and pieces. Now scientists had hundreds of new species, many of them complete skeletons, to study.

The other, more obscure, benefit was the arousal of public interest in these mammoth reptiles, something that had probably never occurred to Cope and Marsh. But there's nothing like the skeleton of an 80-foot-long, 80-ton Brachiosaurus to fire the imagination. It was this interest that paved the way for the preservation of the great dinosaur deposits discovered by Earl Douglas on the Utah-Colorado border. He would have laid a claim to his find. Not good enough, said President Woodrow Wilson, and the deposits became part of Dinosaur National Monument when it was established in 1915.

When you think about great feuds of history—Hatfields and McCoys or Capulets and Montagues—add Cope and Marsh. The world was the winner of that one.

EMPIRE, GEORGETOWN, AND GUANELLA PASS

BOTH Empire and Georgetown lie along or near bustling Interstate 70, so technically neither is in backroads country. But you can't always avoid starting a tour on a major road, and besides you'll miss many interesting places if you do. Like Georgetown, which is also the beginning of a fascinating trip into more remote and scenic country.

If you're heading west from Denver on Interstate 70, however, you'll come to Empire first. Take the turnoff to US Highway 40 and drive two miles to this old mining town. Unlike so many other communities that sprang up where gold was discovered,

Empire survived after the mines played out, becoming an important stage and supply station on the Berthoud Pass route over the Continental Divide. And it's still going strong. While you're in Empire, don't fail to visit Peck House, a 100-year-old hotel complete with antiques and brass beds.

From Empire, you backtrack to Interstate 70 and then continue southwest to the Georgetown exit. To anyone who has lived in Colorado long enough, the name Georgetown usually evokes images of quaint Victorian homes and buildings. Indeed, this once booming mining town has some of the finest

*Hotel de Paris
in Georgetown*

83

examples of late nineteenth-century architecture in the state. Unless you're on an extremely tight schedule, you'll want to spend a while here, exploring the old houses and browsing in some of the shops. When you've satisfied your curiosity, follow the signs in town pointing the way to Guanella Pass.

As you start the upgrade to the pass, don't be dismayed by the warning sign. DO NOT OVERESTIMATE ROAD WIDTH, it warns. (Not me, friend. I have great respect for narrow roads.) After a few switchbacks, you'll come to an overlook with tremendous views of Georgetown and the valley.

The road gains in elevation quite rapidly at first, then the climb is more gradual in a series of looping turns. Typically, the charac-

ter of the forest changes as you approach the higher elevations, with the trees assuming gnarled, stunted forms near wind- and snow-raked timberline.

At Guanella Pass itself (elevation 11,669 feet) are broad vistas of tundra and peaks. Immediately to the southeast is Mount Bierstadt, named for the famous nineteenth-century painter of the Western wilderness, Albert Bierstadt. The mountain's 14,060-foot-high summit blocks the view of Mount Evans. To the west of here are Grays Peak and Mount Wilcox, 14,270 and 13,408 feet in elevation respectively.

To me the outstanding feature of this trip, in addition to the superlative scenery, is the opportunity of seeing one of Colorado's

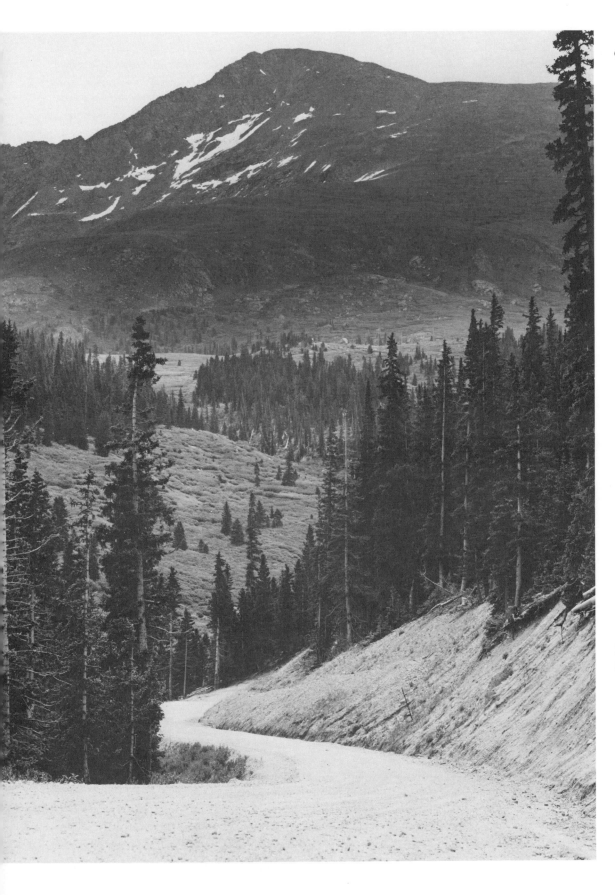

*The road to
Guanella Pass*

BELOW: *Near Guanella Pass*

FACING PAGE: *The Gore Range and the Eagles Nest National Wilderness*

more unusual forms of wildlife, the white-tailed ptarmigan, or "snow grouse." I suspect that even longtime residents of Colorado know nothing about this bird, usually associated with Arctic or semi-Arctic climes. The smallest of the grouse family, ptarmigan live above timberline year round.

Marvelously adapted to this harsh environment, these birds provide a classic example of protective coloration. In winter their plumage and even their eyelids turn completely white to blend with the snow-covered terrain. At the time of year that you are likely to see them in the Guanella Pass

region, their white feathers have been replaced by a mottled gray and brown that blends nicely into the rock-strewn tundra. In fact, as you hike along open expanses above timberline, you may pass several ptarmigan without knowing it. They frequently crouch low to the ground and remain still until you approach within a few feet. This is especially true in the nesting season, during early summer.

Perhaps your best chance of spotting ptarmigan is to park your car at the top of Guanella Pass and walk east or southeast up the gentle slopes of Mount Bierstadt. Even if you don't see one of these alpine denizens, you'll find this rewarding, for the scenery is magnificent and the hike exhilarating.

As the road begins its descent from Guanella Pass, you'll come to several small alpine lakes, then enter forested country again by the Geneva Basin ski area. Lower down, Geneva Creek parallels the road and races along, foaming white, beneath stately old spruce trees. Eventually the road intersects US Highway 285. You can return to the Denver area by turning left. To the right the highway enters the northern part of South Park via 10,000-foot-high Kenosha Pass.

BLACK HAWK AND CENTRAL CITY

COLORADO'S gold rush era. This is where it all began. The funny thing is, it was started by a rumor.

Beginning in 1858 there were widely circulating rumors in the Midwest and East of fabulous gold strikes in the Rockies. The prospectors who hadn't cashed in on California's riches a decade earlier hoped to find their bonanza now. By the fall and winter of 1858, the gold seekers began congregating at the confluence of Cherry Creek and the South Platte River, a site soon to become known as Denver. They came by the dozens, then by the hundreds, waiting for the snows to melt in the High Country. They didn't know it, but the rumors were only partially true: what had actually been discovered were small, scattered placer deposits, hardly the stuff of great fortunes. Then in July, like a self-fulfilling prophecy a rich lode was found in the North Fork of Clear Creek, in the mountains west of Denver, and the gold rush was on. Even by today's standards, the influx to the region was truly astounding. Within months an estimated 20,000 prospectors, entrepreneurs, prostitutes, gamblers, and swindlers flocked to this part of the Front Range, though the harsh mountain winter soon forced many to retreat to the plains of Denver. And when all the surface ore and placer deposits were scoured, corporations were formed to extract the rich ores by hard-rock underground mining. The area was called the "richest square mile on earth," and it fostered the towns of Central City, Black Hawk, and Nevadaville, among others. In all, it yielded more than 75 million dollars in gold. But gradually, even the big mines folded and people moved on, following rumors of great strikes elsewhere.

The best place to start on this tour is in Golden, where you pick up US Highway 6 as it winds west alongside Clear Creek. Once a heavily traveled major route, US 6 has been supplanted in places by Interstate 70 and is now a relatively quiet backroad along this stretch. In about ten miles the highway branches and you take Colorado Highway 119 north, following the North Fork of Clear Creek to the old towns of Black Hawk and Central City. On this part of the trip you can see some of the detrimental aspects of mining, the large dredging piles of lifeless gravel left behind in and alongside the stream.

There is a lot to see in Black Hawk and Central City, and both are thriving tourist attractions. Each of them has numerous back streets and roads leading to old mine sites

FACING PAGE:
*The Colorado River
near Burns*

89

*Bird's-eye view
of Central City*

*Central City
Opera House*

and tailings piles. Central City has restored such marvelous old buildings as the famous Opera House—once considered the finest theater west of the Mississippi—and the Teller House hotel, with its notorious painting, the *Face on the Barroom Floor*. There are some interesting old tombstones in the Dory Hill Cemetery in Black Hawk, and between the two towns a granite monument marks the spot where John H. Gregory made the first gold lode discovery in Colorado. A few miles west of Central City is Nevadaville, formerly a boomtown with a population of several thousand and today a bona fide ghost town.

Extending your trip by continuing south to Idaho Springs, you'll be driving on what is euphemistically called Colorado Highway 279. This is a well-maintained gravel road, but definitely not suitable for large motor homes and trailors or for acrophobics and the fainthearted. Backtrack to Central City from Nevadaville and follow the signs to Idaho Springs. As the road winds slowly up a hillside, you'll have fine panoramic views of this gold boom country. For a fee you can drive in to see the spectacular glory hole—a huge man-made crater, several hundred feet deep and 1,000 feet long, from which millions of dollars in ore was extracted.

*Glory hole
south of
Central City*

*The
Oh-My-God
Road*

The remainder of the highway down into Idaho Springs is what local residents refer to as the "Oh-My-God Road." You'll quickly understand why, for it twists in tortuous switchbacks down steep hillsides. There are no guardrails, and in places the road is so narrow that from the passenger-side windows you can see the steep drop-offs. On a white-knuckle scale of one to ten, Highway 279 ranks about eight in places, but the drive provides magnificent views across Clear Creek Canyon to Mount Evans in the distance, and that makes it worthwhile. Adjacent to Interstate 70, Idaho Springs is an interesting old, as well as a modern-day, mining town. There are more than 100 mines nearby. It's also an old and modern-day tourist resort. The Radium Hot Springs here, which were frequented by the Indians long ago, are still being used by health-seekers.

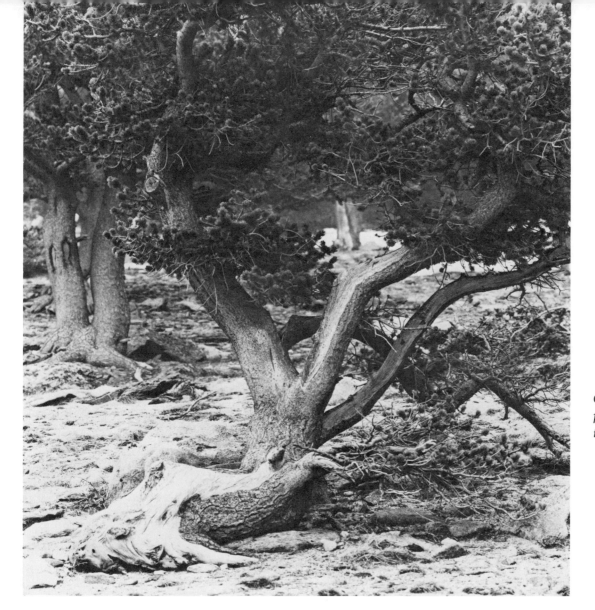

*Gnarled limber
pine along the road
to Mount Evans*

MOUNT EVANS, SQUAW PASS, AND BERGEN PARK

THIS TOUR makes an interesting extension of the Central City trip if you take the "Oh-My-God Road" to Idaho Springs. (If you come into Idaho Springs on Interstate 70, take the Mount Evans exit.)

Colorado Highway 103 leaves Idaho Springs and begins a gradual ascent up the valley formed by Chicago Creek. When nuggets were panned here in the 1860s, this valley—like the Clear Creek Valley to the north—was stampeded by gold seekers. As the road gains in elevation, the character of the forest begins to change. In Clear Creek Canyon around Idaho Springs, the hillsides are dry, and ponderosa pine is the predom-

inant tree species. Not many miles up Chicago Creek, you'll begin noticing mixed stands of spruce and aspen. Higher still are lodgepole pine forests, and as you approach Echo Lake—which is really not even a hamlet, for it has no winter population—the pointed spires of sub-alpine fir become more evident.

At Echo Lake (elevation 10,600 feet) is the beginning of the highest automobile road in the United States—Colorado Highway 5, or the Mount Evans road. It's paved and well maintained, but open only in summer and early fall, for obvious reasons. As you begin climbing in ever-steeper switch-

95

*View east
from the road
to Mount Evans*

backs, the forest continues to change. Soon the alpine fir becomes dwarfed and gnarled from the struggle to survive in this hostile environment. At one of the last turnoffs near timberline, watch for the signs indicating bristlecone pines. These twisted and stunted timberline ancients, found in relatively few places in the world, may be the oldest living things on earth. Biologists have confirmed that some of them are over 4,000 years old.

Leaving behind the last vestige of trees, you are now in the world of alpine tundra. Wild flowers in July and August are spectacular, as are the views from the road down into cirques and into the lake-dotted basins that form the headwaters of Bear Creek to the east. Beyond Summit Lake the road becomes steeper and narrower. After about 12 miles, you arrive at the top of 14,264-foot-high Mount Evans. All along this road, and at the summit, there are excellent opportunities for short hikes to explore the tundra. If possible, you should allow plenty of time to stop and walk around. Among the common tundra flowers are purple moss campion, blue alpine forget-me-not, yellow paintbrush, yellow and white marsh marigold, and the strange purple blossoms of sky pilot, or alpine skunkflower. The latter name is apt, for though the flowers are beautiful, the leaves have a skunklike odor when they are crushed. If you are really ambitious, you might try to get a very early start on the Mount Evans road to watch a magnificent sunrise over the eastern plains.

Back at Echo Lake, Highway 103 leads over 9,807-foot-high Squaw Pass and into the village of Bergen Park. You can catch glimpses from the pass, across the valley of Clear Creek, of the "Oh-My-God Road."

ROCKY

MOUNTAIN

NAT'L

PARK

Longs Peak
+

ESTES PARK

N

4 mi.

⑦

ALLENSPARK

RAYMOND

WARD

BOULDER

㊲

Boulder Cr.

⑲

NEDERLAND

Rollins Pass

ROLLINSVILLE

WINTER PARK

EAST PORTAL

Golden Gate Canyon State Park

⑲

BLACK HAWK

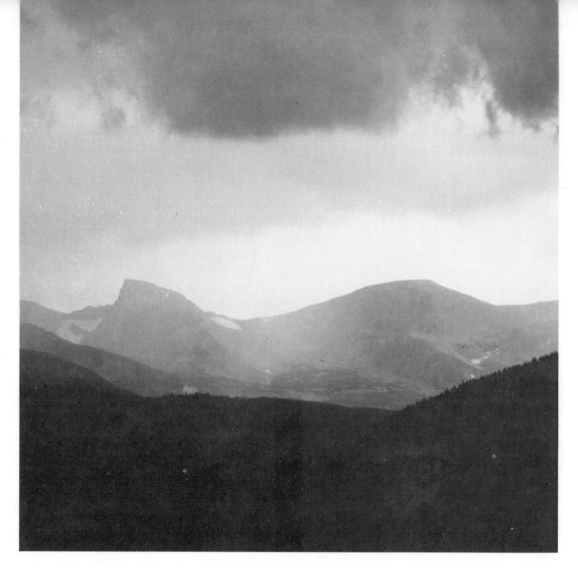

*Storm clouds south
of Rocky Mountain
National Park*

NEDERLAND, ALLENSPARK, AND ESTES PARK

IF YOU choose not to take the "Oh-My-God Road" from Central City to Idaho Springs, the Nederland to Estes Park trip is an ideal extension of the Black Hawk-Central City mini-tour. It's my own favorite route to Rocky Mountain National Park, but be forewarned that the roads are winding and the driving slow. There are several possibilities for side excursions, and the leisurely pace allows you to savor what in my opinion is some of the finest scenery in the Front Range.

From Central City, backtrack to Black Hawk, then turn north on Colorado Highway 119. The road winds through open park-like meadows fringed with aspen forests. About seven miles from Black Hawk turn right for a side trip to Golden Gate Canyon

State Park. There are campgrounds here, and you'll have a great view of the rugged peaks along the Continental Divide to the northwest.

Another interesting side excursion begins in Rollinsville. Take the gravel road left, following signs pointing the way to the village of East Portal. The road parallels the main line of the Denver and Rio Grande Western Railroad. At East Portal is the entrance to a six-mile-long railroad tunnel that cuts under the Continental Divide and emerges near the town of Winter Park. The tunnel replaced the tortuous route over Rollins Pass, now part of the automobile road. The drive over the pass is worthwhile in itself, not only for the scenery but, if you're a railroad buff, also for the marvelous engineering of the wooden railroad trestles. This is an excellent summertime trip if you allow enough time to cross over the Divide to the Winter Park area.

If you backtrack from Rollins Pass or East Portal to Highway 119, you'll continue north through Nederland. The name of this town is derived from the Dutch word meaning "lowland," a seemingly improbable moniker, for Nederland is at an elevation of 8,234 feet. By comparison to the towering mountains west of here, this could of course be termed a lowland. Incidentally, those mountains to the west and northwest are an extension of the massive Front Range that comprises Rocky Mountain National Park to the north.

From Nederland you can take Highway 119 northeast through ruggedly beautiful Boulder Canyon to the city of Boulder or, to continue north, take Colorado Highway 72 through Ward and Raymond, then Highway 7 through Allenspark and eventually to the town of Estes Park, gateway to Rocky Mountain National Park. This portion of the trip is especially scenic and pleasant, with glimpses of Longs Peak—14,256 feet in elevation—along the way.

A word here about Rocky Mountain National Park. I haven't included a description of the park because, technically, it isn't a backroad area. For one thing, there are enormous numbers of visitors here in the summertime. However, in keeping with the general theme of seeking out-of-the-way spots, I suggest that you consider sampling the fine hiking trails in the park. Ranging from a few hours to a few days in duration, these hiking trips will take you to little-known but spectacular places. Rangers at park headquarters can advise you on areas to visit, and maps and trail guides are available here. Hiking is a good way to get away from the crowds. Another alternative is to visit the park in September or early October, well past the peak of the tourist season.

Storm breaking up over Rocky Mountain National Park

Colorado Sketch: ISABELLA L. BIRD

WHEN THE transcontinental railroad was completed in 1869, and a trip out West didn't consist of months on the trail fighting Indians, hunger, and thirst, the tourist business in Colorado started to pick up. The state became a favorite spot for wealthy Englishmen, but as tourists their chief activities seemed to be admiring Western sunsets, shooting buffalo, and sneering at the backward, uncouth natives.

There was one English visitor who was different.

Isabella Bird was a spinster lady of 42, traveling alone that September of 1873, when she stopped off in the Colorado Rockies on her way home to England from the Sandwich Islands (now Hawaii). The embryo Western towns and the cities she hated. The plains, hot and constantly dusty, smothered her. But the mountains, rising clean and pure in an unending line, were like nothing she had ever seen before, and she loved them passionately.

When someone told her about the mountain resort area called Estes Park, she was determined to visit it. Oh, it wasn't for the likes of her, they said. It was hard to get to, it was almost winter in the High Country, and a noted badman lived up there, practically in the park itself. It took two weeks of trying to find a guide, and at least one abortive attempt to get there, before she finally made it.

Estes Park was worth the effort. The scenery was everything Isabella had imagined; the accommodations, while rustic, were agreeable; and the desperado, Mountain Jim Nugent, wasn't such a bad sort after all.

In fact, she got on so well with him that when he suggested a climb up Longs Peak, she readily agreed. The ascent was grueling. Isabella begged several times to be left behind, only to be patiently cajoled, pleaded with, and finally hauled bodily to the 14,256-foot-high summit by Mountain Jim. It was an amazing accomplishment for a cultured, middle-aged Englishwoman of her day. Longs Peak had first been climbed only five years before her ascent.

Isabella now had two loves—the Rocky Mountains and Mountain Jim. However, the first snows had already fallen, and she knew that if she were to see any more of the Colorado mountains, she'd have to leave Estes Park.

She set out on a 600-mile trip that was to take her south to Colorado Springs, west to South Park, and back north to Denver. She became the first—the original—Colorado backroads traveler. Even today, in a car, bad weather can make this a risky trip in November. Isabella did it alone, by horseback, and with no compass. It was an even greater feat than her Longs Peak climb.

There were very few roads as we know them.

She rode through snowstorms and below-zero cold. In places, she had to lead her pony through waist-deep snow. Each night, she faced the same problem—could she find a house whose occupants would be willing to give room and board to her and her horse? But this didn't seem to bother her. She was glad, she said, that there were so few inns because this way she could meet the people.

And meet them she did—everyone from millionaire cattle barons to desperadoes. At one place where she spent the night, she found out later that the body of a hanged man was still in the tree next to the house.

In spite of the hardships, she was happy. She was surrounded by the magnificent mountains, and that was enough. Well, almost enough.

When she returned to Denver, she didn't stay there long. It was back to Estes Park, almost snowbound by now, and Mountain Jim.

This story of the Englishwoman and the mountain man should end with "And they lived

Photo Elliott & Fr.

Isabella Bird Bishop

happily ever after in the mountains they both loved." But it isn't a fairy-tale.

Jim, it seemed, was subject to drunken sprees and "black moods." He couldn't change, and for that matter, neither could Isabella. She wasn't about to give up her adventurous life to become one of those work-hardened pioneer wives of the West. So that was that.

When she returned to England, she published the story of her Colorado adventures in a book called *A Lady's Life in the Rocky Mountains.* Her descriptions of the mountains are eloquent, and her love for them is obvious. She wrote about Jim in a much more restrained manner. She tantalizingly only hints at their mutual deep affection, but then she was marrying someone else, someone back home. Even so that's the way a proper Victorian gentlewoman would write about a love affair, isn't it?

101

THE BLUE RIVER VALLEY AND THE ROAD TO RADIUM

THE FIRST part of the Blue River Valley-Radium trip begins on Colorado Highway 9, which is only marginally a backroad since it is fairly well traveled, especially in the summertime. But the drive is lovely, and it's a convenient way to get to less well-known country in the second part of this tour. After passing through the Eisenhower Memorial Tunnel, Interstate 70 drops steeply down to the town of Dillon, where you take Highway 9 north. The road parallels the Blue River. To the west is the Gore Range, now a part of the Eagles Nest National Wilderness. The Blue River Valley is predominately ranching country. The river itself is a sparkling stream fed by the Dillon Reservoir. There are several

places where you can pull off the highway to try your hand with a trout fly.

About two miles south of Kremmling, just before the road dips down to the Colorado River, keep a sharp eye out for a road leading to the left and a sign pointing toward the village of State Bridge. For the first several miles this road is paved—barely—and climbs open hillsides that give you a fine view of the Blue River Valley, the southern portion of the Gore Range, and the Williams Fork Mountains to the east. The road soon levels out, then begins to descend in winding curves through aspen and spruce forests. At one sharp, final bend there is a magnificent view of the gorge carved by the

Colorado River, and a convenient turnoff allows you to stop for a better look. Almost 1,000 feet below are the white waters of the river. Although here the Colorado is only about 50 miles from its origins near Rocky Mountain National Park, it already has the characteristics of a big, powerful river. The steep gorge upstream is ample evidence.

At this point the road becomes graveled and is carved, literally, from the side of a cliff as it descends to the broad valley below. This isn't spectacular country, but because it is off the general tourist routes, it has a quiet charm. Bright sandstone formations add color, and there are elegant old ranches hidden in thick groves of cottonwoods.

THE BLUE RIVER VALLEY AND THE ROAD TO RADIUM

The Blue River Valley

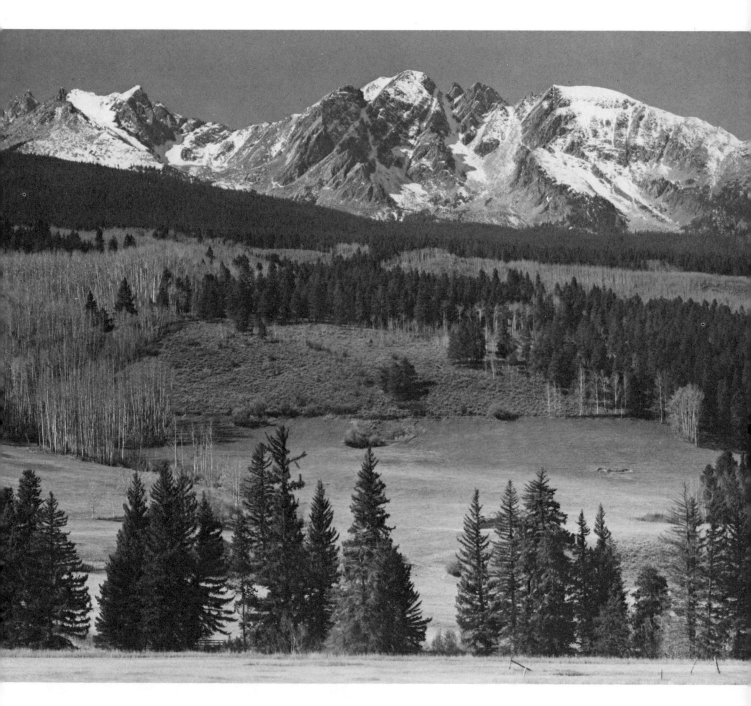

I was intrigued by the name Radium, so I took the marked turnoff, followed a dusty road a few miles north to the Colorado, and crossed an old steel truss bridge over the river. Radium turned out to be a collection of eight or ten rather nondescript houses, with no sign of a store or a public building and no one wandering around of whom to ask how the village got its name. The road leading north into the hills was marked CLOSED, so I didn't try it. There was ample evidence of human habitation here, with cars and pickups parked in front of houses, but not a soul to be seen. I felt as though I had blundered into some calamitous event out of a science fiction movie, the kind in which all the inhabitants of a town have mysteriously disappeared. I retraced my path across the shiny tracks of the Denver and Rio Grande Western Railroad, back across the bridge, then stopped for one last look at Radium. Still no one to be seen. No movement at all across the way. Somewhat later, after doing a little research, I learned that the town was named by a man who thought he'd discovered a radium mine here.

RIGHT: *Ranch
near Radium*

FACING PAGE:
Mount Sneffels

The gravel road continues southwest below colorful sandstone bluffs, then crosses the Colorado about four miles east of State Bridge. At the railroad crossing on the north side of the river I had to wait for a train to pass—one of those long, long freights that took forever. I was the only person on that road for miles and I got stopped by train traffic! But the scenery was pleasant, and I went down to throw rocks in the river as the train crept by.

The road continues southwest and joins Colorado Highway 131 at State Bridge. From here it more closely parallels the Colorado. The mini-tour along this stretch of the river is described next.

ABOVE: *Bridge over the Colorado River near Radium*

FACING PAGE: *Spruce and aspen along the West Dolores River*

*Horses along
the Colorado River
near Burns*

ALONG THE COLORADO RIVER

THERE'S a tendency to forget that the Colorado River has its origins in this state. To many people the river seems more closely associated with the spectacular canyon country of Arizona and Utah than it does with Colorado. But there are more than just traces of the Grand Canyon's character here where the river's still young—not only the stretch between Kremmling and State Bridge (just described) but also west of there, between McCoy and Dotsero.

I had been intending to explore the road from McCoy to Dotsero for years, but I always seemed to be in too much of a hurry on my way to or from somewhere. So there was delicious anticipation when I turned off Colorado Highway 131 a mile or so north of McCoy and followed the signs pointing the way to Burns. Right off I discovered that this is unusual country. For being so close to the high central mountains of Colorado, the area is surprisingly mild and almost desertlike in character, making it a great place to visit in the fall. At any other time of year there is color enough from the sandstone hills and cliffs along the river. But when the golden

108

THE FLAT TOPS

SHORTLY after setting out on this trip, I knew it was going to be special. About two miles north of Dotsero, I turned off the paved road and headed west along the bottom of a steep, narrow canyon formed by Deep Creek. The cottonwoods were at their peak of autumn color, tempting me to stop and camp (it was already late afternoon), but I kept on and soon began to climb steeply in a series of tight switchbacks. For almost an hour I drove steadily upward as the sun sank below the horizon, and it seemed as though the road would never level out. In places it is a long, long way down over that edge of road. Finally, in the twilight of early evening, I reached a plateau and pulled off into a secluded aspen grove. I cooked supper and sipped a cup of wine while watching the soft

amber alpenglow on the mountains to the southeast toward Aspen. Lights glowed in the deep blue shadows of the Eagle River Valley below. The spectacle was made even more superb when a full moon rose out of the Sawatch Range to the southeast. I took a late-night stroll through the faintly lit aspen before turning in.

The next morning was crisp and clear. A light frost lay on the grass as the sunlight slanted through the aspen. I was sitting in the back doorway of the van, sipping my first cup of coffee and enjoying the peaceful scene, when suddenly I heard a noise to my left in the woods. I turned to see a huge bull elk—sleek, fully antlered, and in his prime—edging cautiously toward me about 50 yards away. His breath steamed from his nostrils

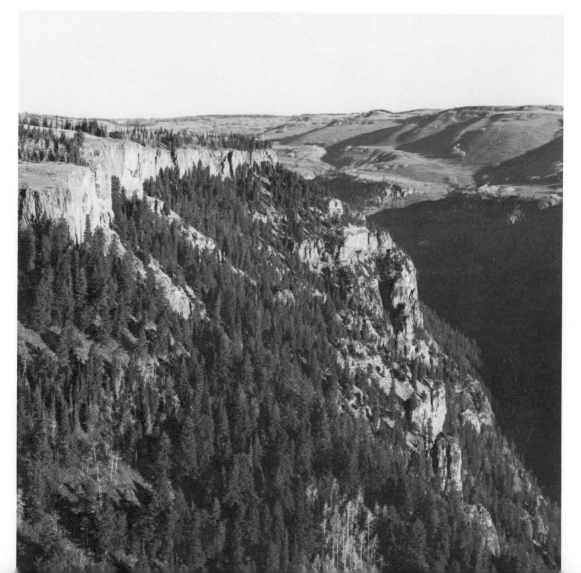

LEFT: *Deep Creek Canyon*

FACING PAGE:
The Colorado River near Dotsero

111

in the cold air. Unfortunately the movement of my head was enough to spook him, and he trotted off rapidly through the aspen with his nose held high and his antlers thrown back to clear the brush. Naturally I didn't have a camera within quick reach. He was gone in a second.

Later I discovered that I had only begun to explore this marvelous road. It winds on for many more miles through vast open country interspersed with groves of aspen and patches of sub-alpine fir. The average elevation here is about 10,000 feet. I'm told that there is an old ghost town known as Carbonate in the area somewhere north of Glenwood Springs. I didn't find it, but I did spot numerous mule deer at the edge of the road.

There is an awesome view of upper Deep Creek, an immense, colorful gorge that is somewhat reminiscent of Utah's Cedar Breaks country. Finally the road ends a few miles beyond Heart Lake, and from here there are trails into the Flat Tops National Wilderness, a 102,124-acre preserve of mountains, rolling hills, forested river valleys, and grassy parks in the White River and Routt national forests. (The Flat Tops are named for an abrupt outcropping of lava in the center of the region.) Because this is a dead-end road, you can have the pleasure of savoring it again on the way out. Magnificent country. I strongly recommend that you allow at least a day, if not two days, to enjoy it fully.

The Western Slopes

TECHNICALLY SPEAKING, THE WESTERN SLOPES begin on the western side of the Continental Divide and thus include a portion of the Rocky Mountain country covered earlier. But because much of the plateau region has a longer traveling season than the high mountain areas, I've limited the Western Slopes section to approximately the western third of the state.

The Western Slope country has a generally different character from the other parts of the state. This is a land of transition between the high alpine peaks of Colorado and the great sandstone and desert country of Utah and Arizona. Dominating features are plateaus, mesas, canyons. The farther west you go, the more arid the land becomes. Instead of cool green forests, you find red and orange sandstone formations, sagebrush, cactus, and junipers.

The Colorado Plateau region is actually a series of 4,000- to 8,000-foot-high plateaus separated by steep-walled canyons. There are mountain ranges in this area also. In fact, a number of Colorado's more than 14,000-foot-high peaks are found here, in the San Juan and San Miguel mountains. To me the appeal of this part of Colorado is the enormous variety of landforms and vegetation. Within hours you can sample alpine tundra, forests, desert, as well as canyons and mesas. Here too are some of the state's wildest rivers: the Colorado, the Dolores, the Gunnison, the Green, and the Yampa. The canyons of the Gunnison, Green, and Yampa are among the world's most spectacular.

For those interested in archaeology or paleontology, the Western Slopes region is a paradise. Near Four Corners, the only point in the United States that is common to four states, places such as Hovenweep National Monument and Mesa Verde National Park offer glimpses into the lives of some of the region's earliest inhabitants—the pre-Columbian ancestors of the present-day Pueblo Indians. It's a fascinating world and one that should be explored at a leisurely pace. At Dinosaur National Monument, two-thirds of which is in Colorado, you can see the fossilized bones of such prehistoric reptiles as Stegosaurus and Brachiosaurus, the latter ranked as the biggest land animal of all time, with a height of 40 feet and a weight of 80 tons. The monument contains the largest deposit of fossilized dinosaur bones anywhere. A visit here provides an insight into Mesozoic and Paleozoic times. And for a look at stark, beautiful geological processes there is Colorado National Monument.

The prime feature of the Western Slopes for the backroads buff is the generally mild climate and possibilities for a relatively early—and late—driving season. Beginning in April, when Colorado's High Country is still locked in the icy grip of winter, you may find it possible to travel many of the backroads in the Western Slopes. You should, of course, check locally about road conditions before taking off. And be apprised of long-range weather forecasts. There's always the chance of being snowed in somewhere during a spring storm unless you heed warnings of impending weather changes.

*The road
from Buford to
New Castle*

THE WESTERN
SLOPES

At the other end of the warm season, fall comes late here. Sometimes there's a range of several weeks, from late September to mid-October, between the peak of autumn color in the High Country and the height of fall in the milder Western Slopes. It's also well past the regular tourist season, so you'll find places quiet and unused.

Rodeo arena in
the White River
Valley

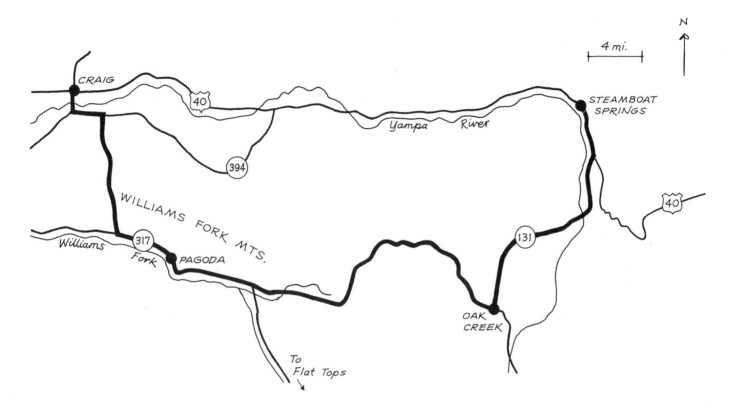

ALONG THE WILLIAMS FORK

I WON'T pretend that this is Colorado's most scenic country. It isn't. But it has a pleasing flavor all its own, even if there are no 14,000-foot-high snowcaps in evidence.

I really don't know what made me decide to take this trip along the Williams Fork. Perhaps I was intrigued by the little dot that represented a place called Pagoda when I was checking out the area on my map. A name like that in itself tends to pique the curiosity. I mean, a lot of Colorado place names reflect the rugged life out here in the early days. Troublesome. Cripple Creek. Fort Wicked. Battle Mountain. Cannibal Plateau. Some names, such as Ouray, Arikaree, Uncompahgre, and Saguache, are direct loans from the Indians; others, such as San Luis, Cortez, and Monte Vista, from the Spanish. Still others, such as Silverton, Telluride, Granite, and Basalt, reflect the mineral wealth or geology of the state. But *Pagoda*?

Well, I had to take a look for myself. I had visions of an exotic Oriental temple, or a facsimile thereof, stuck out here in the middle of nowhere. So I left the town of Craig and followed Colorado Highway 394 south and east for about five miles, then headed straight south on a gravel road. After climbing gradually over some low hills, I descended into the valley of the Williams Fork. Although it was early summer, the scrub oak leaves already looked parched from the heat.

When my road intersected Colorado Highway 317, also graveled, I turned left and made a rough estimate from my map of the remaining distance to Pagoda. Just five miles. The Williams Fork is a lovely stream, whose origins lie in the Flat Tops to the south of here. Along the broad valley are several ranches, one of which seemed a curious combination of Old South and Old West—a huge, two-story log mansion with white-painted balustrade and porch.

Tooling along in a cloud of dust, I must

119

Ranch house near Pagoda

have lost track of time and mileage, for suddenly, flashing past in a blur, something caught my eye. I hit the brakes and skidded to a stop in a spray of gravel and dirt, then backed up. There it was, a boarded-up, broken-windowed old store with a peeling sign—PAGODA. Well, so much for my illusion of finding an ornate temple. There wasn't a clue as to the origin of the exotic name.

I continued on, past the turnoff for the road that heads south to the Flat Tops and the White River. In a little canyon I rounded a bend and saw one of those sheepherder wagons with a horse tied nearby. I stopped

for a picture. When I climbed back into the van, I heard the insistent, unmistakable hissing of a tire going flat. Damn. The road was pretty narrow, and even though I hadn't seen a car yet, I was nervous about changing a tire here. So I continued on, climbing up out of the draw, and stopped on a broad level stretch of road.

As I was finishing my tire-changing chore, a beat-up old pickup truck came roaring out of the canyon and slammed to a stop. When the cloud of dust settled, the old-timer at the wheel asked if he could be of some help. I thanked him and pointed out that I was doing fine, then asked him

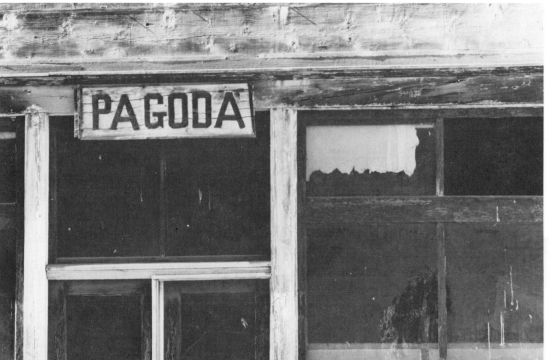

ABOVE: *Sheepherder's wagon in the Williams Fork Valley*

LEFT: *All that remains of the town of Pagoda*

121

about Pagoda. Named for a mountain peak, he said. Back there toward the Flat Tops country. Ah well, there went my final chance for some colorful history.

The last miles of this trip are decidedly unscenic, for there is a huge strip mine (coal) near the town of Oak Creek. I thought about backtracking and taking that road to the south toward the White River, but prudence got the better of me. I turned left on Colorado Highway 131 and headed toward Steamboat Springs to get my tire fixed.

Incidentally, don't confuse the Williams Fork here, which is a branch of the Yampa River, with the Williams Fork of the Colorado. And yes—speaking of place names—there are two Williams Fork Mountains in Colorado. The range in this area though hardly compares with the one in the High Country.

FACING PAGE:
Telluride

BROWNS PARK AND THE GATES OF LODORE

THIS TRIP takes you into the desolate northwest corner of the state, a rugged area carved into deep canyons by the Green and Yampa rivers. At the town of Maybell, turn off US Highway 40 and follow Colorado Highway 318 northwest. Before doing so, however, check your gas supply, for it's a long way to the next service station.

In about nine miles you will cross the broad, sleek Yampa River near Sunbeam. From here north the land is open and dry, with hills covered by junipers, sagebrush, and piñon pines. These stunted and gnarled species of pines were once an important food source for the Indians. Each fall, the women and children gathered the small, sweet nuts in straw baskets. Whenever I'm in piñon country in the fall, I gather some myself, if the squirrels and jays haven't beaten me to them. You may have to settle for a sample, because it takes patience to consume any reasonable quantity. The

LEFT: *The Gates
of Lodore*

FACING PAGE: *Side of
house in Telluride*

125

The Green River near Browns Park and the Gates of Lodore

small, hard shell must be cracked with the teeth before the sweet meat can be extracted. Someone once questioned whether a person could survive in the wilderness on piñon nuts alone, considering their tiny size and the time and energy required to extract the nutritious meat.

About 60 miles from Maybell there's a side road, marked by National Park Service signs, leading into the northernmost tip of Dinosaur National Monument. If you follow this road, you come down to the Green River at a spectacular place called the Gates of Lodore. The name was coined by Major John Wesley Powell during his epic journey down the Green and Colorado rivers in 1869. He took the name from an English poem, "How the Waters Come Down at Lodore," which he would recite as he and his men drifted down the turbulent rivers.

Powell's journey began north of here at the town of Green River, Wyoming, in early May of 1869. It was an amazing feat, charting the largely unknown land and waters of that vast, rugged, inhospitable tableland known as the Colorado Plateau. Not only did the group prove the navigability, albeit difficult in places, of the Green and Colorado rivers, but they made important studies of the geology, flora, and fauna of the region as well. (Powell was a geology professor before he began his career as an explorer.) In late August, the men completed their journey below the great gorges of the Grand Canyon, where Lake Mead is located today. During the course of their trip, reports were widely circulated that the whole party had perished, but Powell eventually returned to Washington a hero. He obtained funds to repeat the trip in 1871 and later became the second director of the United States Geological Survey.

One of the most difficult parts of the journey began here, where the Green River enters a series of steep, narrow defiles at the Gates of Lodore. The group's greatest calamity occurred about ten miles downstream when they lost one of their boats, the "No Name," at a treacherous rapid they subsequently named Disaster Falls. Despite the perils, Powell found much to admire along this stretch of the river. In his now-famous journal, he wrote:

This has been a chapter of disasters and toils, notwithstanding which the Canyon of Lodore was not devoid of scenic interest, even beyond the power of pen to tell. The roar of its waters was heard unceasingly from the hour we entered it until we landed here [Echo Park, at the confluence with the Yampa River]. *No quiet in all that time. But its walls and cliffs, its peaks and crags, its amphitheaters and alcoves, tell a story of beauty and grandeur that I hear yet—and shall hear.*

Continuing north on Highway 318 past the turnoff for the Gates of Lodore, you enter Browns Park, a remote valley that was a favorite hangout of the mountain men in the 1830s and of Butch Cassidy and his Wild Bunch in the early 1890s. Today the valley is a national wildlife refuge, and you'll find it interesting just to wander around here. Both in the spring and in the fall there are large numbers of waterfowl, including Canada geese, whistling swans, sandhill cranes, and several species of ducks. You're also likely to see small herds of pronghorn antelope.

DEERLODGE PARK

COMPARED to the other backroads tours of Colorado, the Deerlodge Park trip is short in distance traveled. But it has such appeal that you'll probably linger for a long while, especially if you make the trip under the same conditions I did.

It was early October when I turned off US Highway 40 between Maybell and Elk Springs and followed the signs toward Deerlodge Park, the southeastern corner of Dinosaur National Monument. The autumn color had long since disappeared from the High Country, but here the cottonwoods were a brilliant orange. It was also well past the

peak of the tourist season, and even US 40 had little traffic on it.

About five or six miles from the highway, after driving through gently rolling sage- and piñon-covered hills, you'll catch your first sight of the Yampa River. The name is derived from the parsniplike plant whose root was a favorite food of the Indians. Each fall several tribes migrated to the Yampa River Valley here in northwest Colorado to collect the nutty, sweet roots. The plant was also well known to early settlers, so much so in fact, that "Yampa" was a contender for the name of the state.

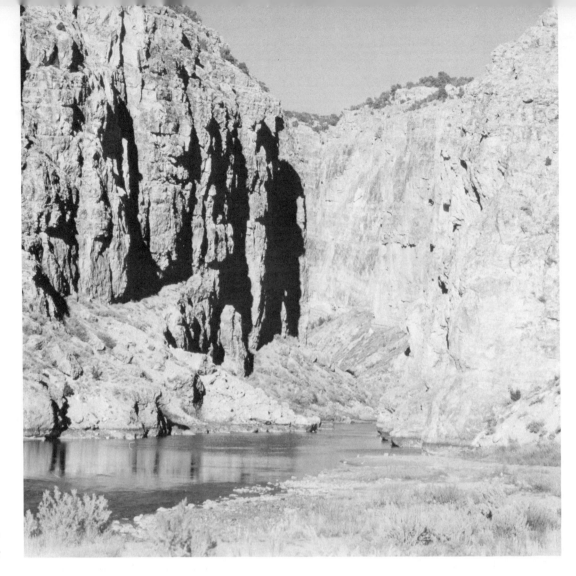

*The Yampa River
near Deerlodge Park*

Pull into the marked scenic area where you first sight the river, for there is a breath-taking view of the gorge carved by the water. Here the Yampa emerges from between steep, sheer walls and meanders lazily through a broad valley for several miles before plunging into a series of great gorges to the west.

The road ends in another nine miles, just after entering Dinosaur National Monument. There is a small but lovely camp-ground here, in a grove of huge cottonwood trees. This spot is so relaxing and inviting, you'll probably want to stay awhile. And that's what I did. I expected to see at least one or two other cars pull into the camping area before nightfall, but I had the place to myself. In fact, I never saw another soul that afternoon or the next day. As the sun dipped toward the sandstone rim beyond the camp-ground, I cooked a small supper and enjoyed the play of twilight colors on the cotton-woods. My tranquil mood was somewhat disturbed, however, when two magpies flew into a nearby cottonwood and took up a silent vigil for food morsels. Magpies are generally cautious birds, but these two seemed like old hands at campground larceny. As I sat there eating my canned stew and sipping wine from a tin cup, they glided down past the table for a closer look, landing on the ground only a few feet away from me. I tossed them a small piece of French bread and they pounced on it. After a brief squabble, one of the birds flew off with the tidbit. The other waddled indignantly over to me and demanded its share. I responded, and it too flew off with a small piece of bread.

I quickly realized that my generosity had been a mistake. In a few minutes the pan-

*Cottonwoods
in Deerlodge Park*

*Mule deer
in Deerlodge Park*

handlers were back. Even worse, they brought their whole gang with them, and soon there were almost a dozen magpies in the cottonwood, squawking loudly in threatening, demanding tones. I felt as though I had been thrust into the middle of a scene from Alfred Hitchcock's movie *The Birds*. Trying to eat with dozens of greedy eyes watching was a bit uncomfortable, so I hastily finished my repast and went for a walk in the parklike grove of cottonwoods, swishing my feet through the litter of leaves. Three mule deer bounded up a sage-covered hillside, then stopped and stared at me while their ridiculous ears flopped incessantly to ward off a few bugs. It was nearly dark when I got back to the campground, and most of the magpies were gone. I threw a sleeping bag on the ground and slept out under a clear sky, riddled with stars.

Next morning there was frost on the ground. I had a quick cup of tea, then went for another hike as the sun slanted through the trees and melted the frost. I made friends with several more mule deer before firing up the van for the drive back to US 40. Didn't see anyone all the way back to the highway. A good spot to get away from it all.

THE VALLEY OF THE WHITE RIVER

IN 1868, the year before he made his epic journey down the Green and Colorado rivers, Major John Wesley Powell led an overland expedition down the valley of the White River. He later wrote, " . . . the region is one of great desolation: arid, almost treeless, with bluffs, hills, ledges of rock, and drifting sands."

Powell's description is perhaps better suited to that portion of the White River near its confluence with the Green, for the section from Meeker to Rangely along Colorado Highway 64 is quite beautiful. True, the surrounding hills are dry and desertlike, but the bottomlands are lush and fertile, with mag-

nificent old cottonwoods scattered along the riverbanks.

I began the tour in Meeker a few miles west of the intersection of Colorado highways 789 and 132. The town was named for Nathan C. Meeker, an inept but well-meaning Indian agent who in 1879, along with nine other employees of the White River Agency, was killed by his charges, the northern Utes, in a revolt his blunderings incited. The intervention of Ouray, an articulate and intelligent chief of the southern Utes (described next), prevented more bloodshed. About three miles west of here, just off Highway 64, is a monument marking the spot

The White River

*Abandoned
schoolhouse along
Colorado
Highway 64*

where the fight, known today as the "Meeker Massacre," took place. (This is the same Meeker who in 1870 had founded the town of Greeley, described later.)

About 20 miles west of Meeker, Highway 64 is intersected by an unmarked road, a drive along which makes a worthwhile trip. Running south and east for 30 miles, the route parallels Piceance Creek. (*Piceance* is a Ute word meaning "tall grass.") The road winds through towering sandstone bluffs in the heart of the mountain-plateau-desert transition region of Colorado. Today the area is the center of an environmental contro-

versy, for this is oil shale country and there is considerable concern over the potential harm to the land by strip mining. Fortunately, with cheaper and more ecologically sound energy alternatives emerging, full-scale development of these oil shales seems deferred, at least for now. The road ends at the town of Rio Blanco near the southwestern corner of the Flat Tops. Turn left here on Highway 789 to return to Meeker.

If you chose not to take the Piceance Creek side trip, however, you can continue west on Highway 64 through more of the verdant White River Valley to Rangely.

Colorado Sketch: CHIEF OURAY

EVERY once in a while a great statesman comes along. Sometimes, if he's in the right spot at the right time, he can change history. Sometimes, history just flows right over him like an unchecked tidal wave, and such was the case with the Ute Indian chief Ouray.

Some say the fact he was born in 1833, the year of one of the most fantastic meteorite displays in history, was an omen that he was destined for greatness. His upbringing certainly had a lot to do with his career as a statesman. Born of an Apache father and a Ute mother, he was reared in the household of a loving Spanish family near Taos, New Mexico. By the time he rejoined the Uncompahgre Utes as a teenager, he spoke several languages and was at home with three of the major cultures of the Southwest—Spanish, Anglo, and Ute. Unknowingly, he had been trained for statesmanship as carefully as any prince is trained for ruling a country.

Given this background, Ouray probably had more insight into what was going on in the West than the average person of his time. And what he observed happening to the Indians he didn't like. A trip through the newly discovered goldfields near Denver increased his concern. It would be only a matter of time, he felt, before the hordes of gold- and land-crazy white men would take over all the Indian lands in Colorado.

It was clear to Ouray, who was by now chief of the Uncompahgre Utes, that the Indians needed a treaty outlining what lands were to be theirs. In 1863 such a treaty was signed. The Utes were granted all of the Colorado land west of the Continental Divide "forever," but they agreed to give up mineral rights to the territory in exchange for 20,000 dollars' worth of goods annually for ten years.

In five years, under pressure from Colorado mining interests, Washington was ready to write another treaty. Actually, so was Ouray. He had formulated a new plan for all the Colorado Utes and was chosen to be their spokesman at the treaty table.

First, he'd make sure they had a reservation of their own, land no white man could take away from them. Then, he'd gradually wean the Utes from their strictly hunting economy and develop one that would allow them to survive in the modern world. The new Indian economy would include stock raising and increased trade with the whites. And with honest Indian agents on the reservation to assure that the annuities granted by the government would not consist of spoiled supplies, the Utes should be able to manage quite well.

If Washington thought Ouray would be a pushover at the treaty talks, they were dead wrong. The Indians came out on top. The treaty of 1868 gave them a reservation of 16 million acres on the Western Slopes of Colorado—far more than the small southwestern corner of the state that the politicians wanted to cede them. The reservation would have two agencies: the White River Agency for the use of the northern Utes and the Los Piños Agency for the southern Utes. The Indians were also to get 50,000 dollars' worth of supplies every year. Furthermore—and perhaps most important—white settlers and miners were specifically prohibited from passing through the Ute territory. Ouray had succeeded in attaining the first part of his economic goal.

Meanwhile, back in the goldfields, there were bigger and better strikes. When gold was discovered in the San Juan Mountains, miners flocked there by the hundreds. The fact that this was Ute land didn't bother them a bit, but it did bother the Utes. Obviously, something had to be done.

It was. In 1873 Ouray and representatives of all the other Ute nations met with a special Indian Bureau commission. The result was the Brunot Treaty, which ceded 4 million acres of the San Juan Mountains back to the whites for 25,000 dollars a year and hunting privileges. The lust for gold had won.

*Chief Ouray
and his wife,
Chipeta*

Ouray knew that this treaty was the only way short of warfare—which would be genocidal—to keep the Utes from being pushed out of Colorado altogether. His biggest task now was to try to prevent any Ute hotbloods from precipitating an incident that would give the whites an excuse to rescind all the hard-fought treaties and move the Utes to some godforsaken land outside of Colorado. It would not be easy.

While Ouray was admired and respected by both whites and Indians for his statesmanship, he had made some enemies in his rise to power. And as one chief among many, he had never been able to speak for all Indians any more than the governor of one state can speak for all Americans. The dissidents viewed the Brunot Treaty as evidence that Ouray and the other chiefs who had agreed to it had sold out to the whites. The northern Utes from the White River Agency especially gave Ouray nightmares.

Six years after the signing of the Brunot Treaty, everything Ouray had worked for collapsed. Given the anti-Indian temper of the times and the growing "Utes must go" sentiment, it's amazing it took that long for the precipitating incident to occur. But it's not surprising that when it did, it happened at the White River Agency.

Nathan C. Meeker, honest but idealistic to a fault, was appointed Indian agent of the northern Utes. He was absolutely determined that for their own good his Utes would give up hunting for agriculture. The Indians were not particularly interested in becoming farmers, but they humored him until he did the unpardonable. He plowed up their pony racetrack and pony pasture. They were as furious as present-day Denverites would be if someone plowed up Mile-High Stadium, home of the Denver Broncos.

As the tension between whites and Indians mounted, Meeker called for military protection. In response to the advance of the troops, the northern Utes burned the agency buildings; killed all the white men at the post, including Meeker; and took Meeker's daughter, wife, and another white woman and her two small children captive.

Ouray was heartsick. He sent a message to the northern Utes calling for the end of hostilities. His action and the arrival of more troops brought about an end to the fighting. Then he helped negotiate for the release of the captives, thinking perhaps if they were returned unharmed, it would help the Utes' cause.

A month later the hostages were released but by then nothing could help the Utes, particularly after the women revealed that the Indians had taken certain "liberties" with them.

Still, Ouray tried. Although sick with nephritis, he went to Washington to try to get the best possible terms for his people in the renegotiation of territorial treaties and to keep a government investigating committee from being too harsh with the guilty Utes.

Then he accepted the thankless task of getting his people to sign the treaty that would move them to three new reservations. One of these was in Utah, and the second on the New Mexico-Colorado border. The third reservation was to be located around the confluence of the Colorado (at that time called the Grand) and Gunnison rivers near present-day Grand Junction, if suitable land could be found there.

Ouray died in August 1880. He was 48. A year later—no suitable land having been found near Grand Junction—his people were herded to a new reservation in Utah. Only a band of southern Utes remained in Colorado, on a small strip of land in the southwest corner of the state, with a still smaller section extending into New Mexico.

Chief Ouray was not forgotten. In 1900 it was decided to choose 16 people from the ranks of famous Colorado citizens of the past to comprise a state Hall of Fame. Their portraits, done in stained glass, would adorn the dome of the new Capitol. Chief Ouray was the second person chosen for the honor.

NEW CASTLE TO BUFORD

I TURNED off Interstate 70 at New Castle—an old mining camp named for the well-known English coal mining town—because I was curious about the backroad shown on my map that heads north to Buford through a part of the White River National Forest. This is the western edge of the Flat Tops country (described earlier), and I anticipated some great scenery. I wasn't disappointed.

A few miles north of New Castle the paved road becomes graveled as it begins to climb gradually out of the farming and ranching valley of Elk Creek. (How many Elk Creeks are there in the West, I wondered. In my travels in the Rockies I'll bet I have seen, drunk from, crossed, or fallen into more than a hundred of them. The same is true of Bear Creeks, Rattlesnake Creeks, and Deer Creeks.) In about ten miles I entered the northwestern unit of the White River National Forest. Established in 1891 to pre-

serve the scenic resources around the headwaters of the White River, the National Forest experienced a devastating infestation of spruce bark beetles a few decades ago. In many places here there are silvery, ghostlike remains of the dead trees still standing. Though severe at times, such infestations of tree-killing beetles are now understood by ecologists to play a role in long-term forest ecology by thinning extremely dense stands of trees and opening up areas for eventual replacement by other tree species. I saw some stands of dead spruce on this trip, but for the most part, the forest seemed fully recovered and healthy.

After climbing steeply, the road levels out and for miles transverses rolling parklike country, the vast swales of grass interspersed with coniferous forest. In several places there are beautiful views of the Roan Plateau and the ridge called Grand Hogback.

137

*View west from
the Buford-to-
New Castle road*

THE WESTERN
SLOPES

BELOW: *The White
River Valley
near Buford*

FACING PAGE:
*Dunton and the
West Dolores River*

A number of side roads along this route lead to trail heads for trips into the Flat Tops National Wilderness. There are several US Forest Service campgrounds here, and I stopped for lunch at one of them. Two gray-white Canada jays, or "camp robbers," flew down from a nearby tree and insisted on sharing my peanut butter and jelly sandwich. These large and handsome birds are quite familiar in most Colorado campgrounds. They've become expert panhandlers; in fact, they are so brazen at times that they will literally eat out of your hand.

Heading north through the forest again, I came over a small rise and spotted something crossing the road in the distance. As I approached, it darted into the forest. When

I got closer, I stoppped. Then I saw a gray-brown form loping casually through the trees—a coyote. It halted for a moment to check me out, its ears standing sharply erect and pointed, its eyes fixed on me. Then it turned and disappeared into a draw. I left with a nice feeling, knowing that at least a few coyotes around here hadn't been hunted, poisoned, or trapped.

Eventually the road descends into the quiet and peaceful valley of the White River. In the town of Buford it intersects Colorado Highway 132. Continuing to the right on an unmarked road, you can reach Trappers Lake and another part of the lovely Flat Tops country. I turned left and headed toward Meeker.

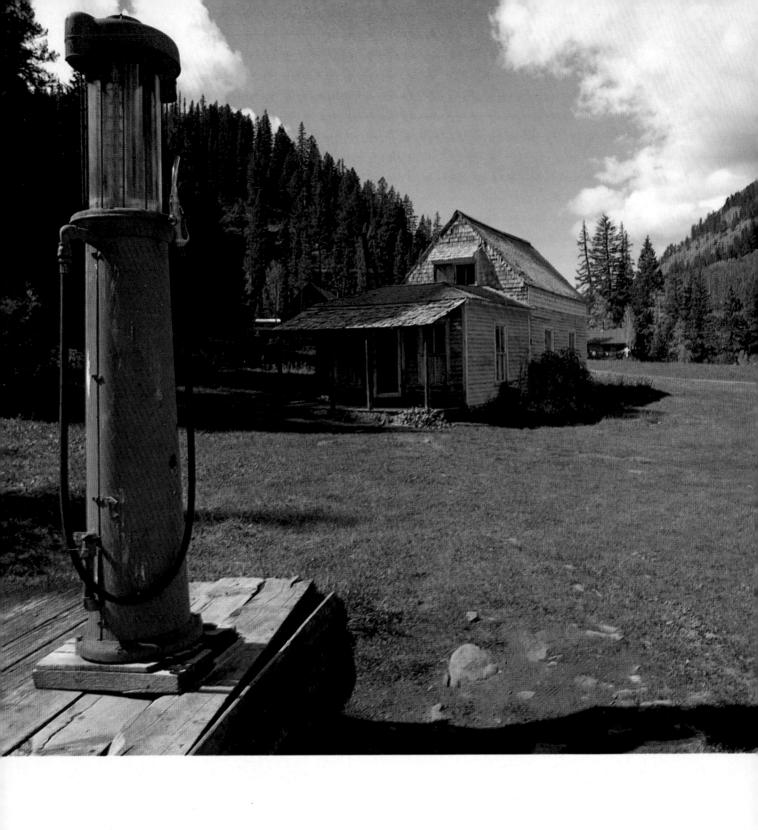

GRAND MESA

ONE OF western Colorado's most prominent landforms, Grand Mesa is indeed grand. This 50-square-mile flat-topped plateau rises more than 5,000 feet above the bordering Gunnison and Colorado River valleys. With an elevation of between 10,000 and 11,000 feet above sea level, the mesa's climate and vegetation vary enormously from its base to its top. In the lowlands of the Gunnison and Colorado rivers, the average annual precipitation is only about eight inches, whereas the cooler plateau top receives about 30 inches and lies deeply blanketed in snow much of the year. The result of these extremes in climate and weather is a remarkable series of vegetative zones in a relatively short distance. In climbing toward the summit of Grand Mesa by any one of four roads, you pass through four distinct biological regions: the Upper Sonoran, Transitional, Montane, and Sub-alpine zones, representing the equivalent encountered in a journey of several thousand miles northward. For anyone interested in geology, a trip to the top of the vast mesa provides a fascinating look at a record of sedimentary strata and the effects wrought by ancient vulcanism and the forces of wind and water.

I began my own Grand Mesa trip northeast of Grand Junction where US Highway 6 crosses the Colorado River just east of De Beque. Heading west watch for an obscure road on the left with a sign pointing the way to Mesa. The road begins as a blacktop but soon becomes graveled. My reason for choosing this particular route (there are more

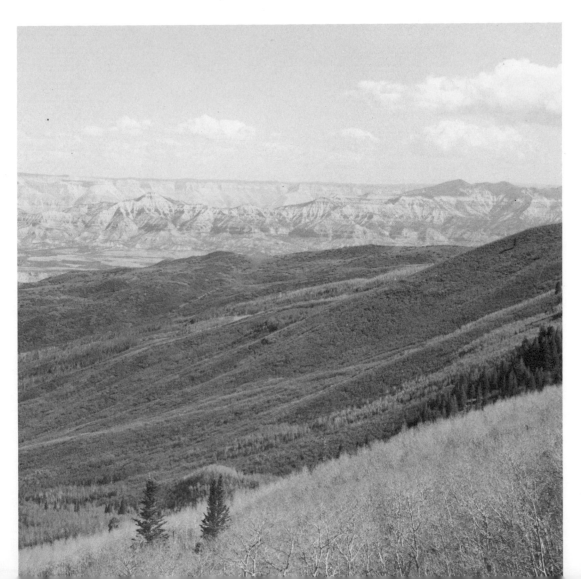

LEFT: *View north from near the top of Grand Mesa*

FACING PAGE: *Dunton*

143

direct approaches) was one of those symbols on my road map that indicate unusual features. In this case it said "Paintpot Country." Being a backroad freak, I was compelled to check it out. However, darkness began to close in on me soon after I turned off the main highway, so I pulled off the dirt road into a sandy draw and camped amid some fragrant piñon pines, junipers, and sagebrush.

The next morning I continued on my trek, heading south, and soon discovered the origin of the name on the map. This is incredibly austere country of sandstone buttes eroded into creased hills, carved canyons, and stone towers, all in multicolored hues ranging from slate gray to white to buff to orange to deep maroon. As I neared the intersection of Colorado Highway 65, I also got my first glimpse of Grand Mesa. Rising abruptly above a sea of green forest, it was rimmed along its flat top by snow.

The next portion of the trip took me through the lovely hamlet of Mesa on Highway 65. Soon the road begins to climb in gradual, sweeping curves up the plateau's northern edge, and during the ascent there's another of those transitions in season. The valley around Mesa was hot and summery when I was there (it was late in May). As

Waterfall and ice-covered trees and rocks on Grand Mesa

145

the road gained in altitude, the deep green foliage of the aspen was replaced by a lighter, fresher verdancy, then brown buds, then totally bare branches near the mesa top. As I drove along the flat summit through dark coniferous forests, snow lay deep in shady places and some of the lakes were rimmed with ice. Farther south toward the interior of the mesa, the snow became deeper alongside the road, lakes were frozen, and a brisk, cold wind let you know that it was still winter here.

South of Skyway (a resort and a few stores) I turned right, taking the marked turnoff to Lands End—intrigued by the name. The dirt road winds through meadows and sparse forests, touched here and there with the incipient green of spring. Apparently this area closest to the mesa's western edge has a more moderate climate than the interior because of the warm westerly winds raised from the mild valley below. But as I was about to discover, the wind on this particular day was far from warm.

Approaching the rim of the mesa near

Shirttail Point, I spotted an unusual phenomenon: trees and rocks coated thickly with ice. The source, I found, was a waterfall that plunged over the mesa's lip and was whipped into spray by cold winds. I got out to photograph the scene, only to discover that the winds were no gentle zephyrs funneling up from the valley below. I literally had to hold the camera and tripod down in order to take a picture, and in the time it took to accomplish this task, I nearly suffered frostbite! I later estimated the air temperature to be a few degrees above freezing, but the wind velocity of well over 50 miles per hour (a conservative estimate) made the chill factor the equivalent of about zero.

At Lands End the road descends 5,000 feet in a series of spectacular switchbacks. The views of the Gunnison Valley and the distant Grand Valley around Grand Junction are superb. And when I arrived at US Highway 50, in the valley once more, the temperature was nearly 80. This trip ranks among the most beautiful, exciting, and varied of my backroads tours of Colorado.

Looking northwest from Shirttail Point toward the Grand Valley

Colorado Sketch: ESCALANTE AND DOMÍNGUEZ

AS THE literature published during the US Bicentennial occasionally pointed out, there were other events besides the signing of the Declaration of Independence that took place in July, 1776. While those earnest colonists in Philadelphia were drafting the document that would end British domination in the East, a band of equally earnest men in Santa Fe, New Mexico, were preparing an expedition designed to ensure Spanish domination in the West.

The Spanish were the earliest white settlers in the Southwest, but just being first didn't mean much. You had to hold on once you were there. And the Spanish remembered that their missionaries and soldiers had been pushed out of the area by an uprising of the Pueblo Indians, if only temporarily. Now, the Spanish authorities in the New World were getting increasingly nervous about the English, French, and Russian explorations of the far West. Finding a route that would connect the remote settlements in New Mexico to the missions in California for the purposes of communication and defense was considered to be of the utmost importance.

The men chosen for the job were two Franciscan friars—Fray Silvestre Vélez de Escalante and Fray Francisco Atanasio Domínguez. Escalante had had a little experience in the exploring business—13 days the previous year spent visiting the Moqui (Hopi) Indian pueblos and trying to get to the Grand Canyon of the Colorado.

Escalante and Domínguez led their band of eight men out of Santa Fe on July 29, 1776. When they reached a place near the site of present-day Pagosa Junction, they had crossed into territory that exactly 100 years later would become Colorado. From there the route they followed would take them through some of the roughest—and some of the most beautiful—terrain in Colorado.

The first part of their course had been explored before, by Juan Maria Rivera in 1765. One of Rivera's men was now with the Escalante group as the official guide. He led them to the Dolores River and its steep-sided canyon. They had a little trouble getting across it. They seemed always to be either too high above the water, or too confined in the bottom of the canyon.

By the time the group had reached the even more difficult, barren canyon country around the present-day town of Bedrock, they figured they'd better give up on the "official" guide and find an Indian one. Heading east, they entered the Uncompahgre Valley and then followed the North Fork of the Gunnison. At this point they finally found a guide. It took a bit of persuasion—the other Indians thought they were crazy to continue.

The party traveled over the top of Grand Mesa, went down its northern side, and came to the Colorado River near what is now De Beque. Here the Colorado is just another river and was easy to cross.

Heading northwest through the Roan Plateau to the White River at present-day Rangely and then west, they entered Utah. Continuing west to Utah Lake the group turned south to Sevier Lake and finally came to the Virgin River in the southwestern corner of Utah.

By now it was winter, complete with snow. Discretion won over valor, and Escalante and Domínguez decided to turn back to Santa Fe. But rather than trying to retrace their circuitous route, they attempted a shortcut straight east.

This meant they would have to recross the Colorado River, which would prove to be a truly terrifying experience. That innocent little river they had crossed in Colorado was a torrent at the bottom of the Grand and Glen canyons in Arizona and Utah.

They tried to ford the river at what is now Lees Ferry, Arizona, just south of the Utah border, but couldn't make it. Climbing back up to the rim, they traveled along the north side of Glen Canyon and finally, at a point that would ever after be known as "The Crossing of the Fathers," found a place where they could swim across.

They had no idea how lucky they were to have found that spot. Major John Wesley Powell, after his famous trip down the Colorado River 90 years later, said he knew of only two places in 500 miles where the river could be reached from the rim—Lees Ferry and The Crossing of the Fathers.

After this ordeal, the rest of the trip to Santa Fe must have seemed easy. The party arrived home on January 2, 1777. From this point on the careers of the two friars became obscure, and they disappeared from history. We're not even sure when they died.

Escalante and Domínguez had not found a route from Santa Fe to California, so their superiors undoubtedly considered them colossal failures. But were they?

They had traveled 2,000 miles over extremely difficult terrain in five months, exploring a huge inland region that had heretofore been virtually ignored. And the route they followed did eventually serve as the basis for part of the Old Spanish Trail, which went from Santa Fe to California.

Escalante had kept a meticulous journal during the expedition. In the days when many explorers looked upon a rugged landscape as something to be endured and conquered, Escalante saw beauty in it. His descriptions reveal his great appreciation of the magnificent rivers, mountains, and forests in the areas through which his party traveled. His reports of the journey are valued by historians. The world should have more of these "failures."

VANCORUM TO GRAND JUNCTION

THE TERRAIN through which you drive on this trip, from Vancorum to Uravan to Gateway to Grand Junction by way of Colorado Highway 141 and US Highway 50, bears a striking resemblance to that of Monument Valley and certain other parts of northern Arizona. It seems impossible that the weirdly carved landscape could be part of Colorado—impossible, that is, if you visualize the state's scenery as consisting solely of forested slopes, snowcapped mountains, and prairie.

You can begin the trip at Grand Junction or, as I did, at Naturita, on Colorado highways 141 and 90. Vancorum is about two miles northwest of here, and just beyond the town Highway 141 becomes a scenic route. The road parallels the San Miguel River for about ten miles, then runs along the Dolores after the two rivers merge north of Uravan. (Uravan is named for the uranium and vanadium mined and refined in the region.) Over eons of time, the water has cut a steep

gorge in the brilliant red and orange sandstone. Following the course of the rivers, you'll have superb views of the canyon and the surrounding countryside.

A few miles north of Uravan is a turnoff and overlook. Here you can see the remnants of an old wooden flume on the sheer walls of the canyon below. Built in the early 1890s, the six-mile-long wooden channel was intended to carry water to some arid, gold-bearing placer deposits downstream. Workmen were lowered in cradles from the canyon rim to affix the wooden trough to the vertical walls of the cliff. Although 173,000 dollars were spent on the project, it was abandoned after a few years because the deposits yielded little gold. Today parts of the old flume cling precariously to the canyon walls as a monument to gold-crazed perseverance.

Between Uravan and Gateway the canyon alternates between a steep, narrow gorge and a broad, open valley where the Dolores meanders placidly. The brown, sediment-laden waters of the river are fringed by feathery, lavender-blossomed tamarisks and by cool, green cottonwood trees. It is in this section that the scenery becomes so reminiscent of northern Arizona. Great sandstone buttes and mesas rise hundreds of feet above the valley. Erosion has created numerous towers and stone goblins in a variety of shapes. Side canyons invite a short hike to see what mysteries lie beyond the first bend. (Some ancient cliff dwellings? Cool, shaded alcoves? Perhaps a deep, cold spring beneath a towering wall?) Incipient arches in the form of conchoidal depressions lie at the bases of smooth, orange walls. Along the highway

and the river's edge wave blossoms of scarlet gilia, orange globe mallow, and yellow princess plume. The area is a perfect example, in all its geological and biological forms, of the great slickrock country of the vast Colorado Plateau country.

At Gateway the highway heads northeast, leaving the Dolores River, which plunges on into a series of canyons before joining the Colorado River. This section of the road passes through Unaweep Canyon—which is also colorful sandstone country—then the landscape makes a subtle transition as you climb gradually up the northern edge of the Uncompahgre Plateau. Green cultivated fields of farms and ranches contrast

*The Dolores River
Canyon north
of Uravan*

149

*The Dolores River
near Gateway*

with the brilliant rocks. But soon the red sandstone is replaced by more austere brown and gray tones. Finally, white and buff sandstone walls line the road as you descend the last few miles to US 50 at Whitewater, southeast of Grand Junction in the broad, arid valley of the Gunnison River.

From Whitewater it's a short distance to Grand Junction, where you have the opportunity to take an interesting side trip to Colorado National Monument, a 28-square-mile area of grotesquely carved and fantastically colored sandstone canyons and monoliths. You really shouldn't pass this up. At Grand Junction turn off onto Colorado Highway 340 for the ten-mile drive that leads directly to the monument's northern entrance. There's a campground close by if you want to relax a bit before continuing, for an exciting 22-mile automobile ride, along Rim Rock Drive, lies ahead of you. Parking overlooks are located to provide views of the most unusual sandstone formations. The highlight of the drive on this road is the steep, serpentine ascent (known as the Trail of the Serpent) up to aptly named Cold Shivers Point on the brink of a precipice 1,000 feet deep. Rim Rock Drive runs into Highway 340, which takes you back to Grand Junction.

UNCOMPAHGRE PLATEAU

IN A SENSE, the Uncompahgre Plateau might be termed a Grand Mesa that didn't quite make it. Or perhaps it's still in the making. Raised above the surrounding region by gradual uplifting, the plateau is nearly as high and as flat as Grand Mesa. However, erosion forces over eons of time have smoothed the edges of the tableland so that its contours are less jagged and, from most approaches, less spectacular than those of its counterpart 40 miles away, across the Gunnison Valley. But this area has a beauty and grandeur of its own. (If you are wondering about the odd name, it is derived from a Ute Indian word meaning "red water canyon" or, according to other interpretations, "stinking waters.")

In the town of Delta—near the convergence of the Gunnison and Uncompahgre rivers—take Colorado Highway 348. (The

Roubideau Canyon

The Uncompahgre Plateau near Columbine Pass

signs here point the way to Nucla.) About six miles southwest of the town the highway turns sharply left, but you should continue straight ahead on the unmarked road and follow the Uncompahgre National Forest access signs. In these first few miles of the trip, you might spot evidence of an unusual problem for this agricultural area (Delta is in the center of the state's largest fruit-growing region). Underlying a large part of the valley and of the Grand Valley to the north are deposits of salt-laden Mancos shale. Gradually, leeching of the salt and its deposition on bottomlands result not only in soil with a high alkalinity but also in such a concentration of salt that the deposits can actually be seen as white encrustations on some of the farmland. Scientists are currently working on methods of halting and reversing this salt buildup, which ultimately destroys the land's productivity.

The road soon climbs above the farmlands and enters a zone of extreme aridity. So sparse is vegetation that the land here resembles a moonscape in places. But almost immediately some of the region's most striking features come into view. On the left is Roubideau Canyon, an eroded and colorful sandstone gorge resembling a scaled-down Grand Canyon. A stream winds through the canyon bottom and lush grasses and cottonwoods contrast with the surrounding barren land. (An inviting place for some future exploration, I noted.) On the right the land drops away steeply into Cottonwood Canyon, not quite as deep as Roubideau but equally colorful.

Gradually more vegetation appears alongside the road: piñon pine and juniper, then scrub oak. Finally you enter the fringes of coniferous forests mixed with stands of aspen. For miles the majestic white-barked trees line the road, and here and there you pass an old ranch with rail fences of aspen stacked in a zigzag pattern.

At Columbine Pass (elevation 8,500 feet) the road divides. Turn left—the road to the right leads to Unaweep Canyon and to the northernmost edge of the plateau described earlier—and in a mile or so turn right following the signs to Nucla. (Taking the second road left when you leave Columbine Pass will lead you to a juncture with Colorado Highway 90 and northeast to Montrose.)

As the road to Nucla begins its descent of the southwestern edge of this vast mesa, there are superb views of Lone Cone Peak far to the south. Lone Cone is a 12,613-foot snowcapped pyramid jutting skyward over the land like a lonely sentinel.

Right away you'll note a difference

between the western and eastern flanks of the Uncompahgre Plateau. The western side apparently receives much more moisture, for the land is far less austere and there is a considerable variety of vegetation all the way to the valley floor near Nucla. It seems likely that, because of its great size and relative height, the Uncompahgre Plateau influences weather patterns of the region. Air masses blown in by prevailing westerly winds are raised and chilled, causing them to release moisture as rain and snow. This "wringing" effect in the west leaves the eastern and northern parts of the plateau more arid.

Crossing some streams dammed by beavers, the road dips into a valley, then ascends a rise before dropping down into the lush farmlands of the San Miguel Valley, where it intersects Colorado Highway 141.

OWL CREEK PASS

IT WAS spring—early May as I remember—when I set out to explore the Owl Creek Pass region east of the Uncompahgre Valley. I had been on the road for several days on a shooting assignment, documenting environmental problems in certain parts of Colorado, and frankly, I was tired of photographing junkyards, litter, and pollution. Time to capture some of Colorado's beauty as well, I thought. So as I was tooling south on US Highway 550 on my way toward Ouray, I got hooked by that old backroad syndrome when I spotted a dirt road leading left and a sign that said OWL CREEK PASS. The road begins where Colorado Highway 62 ends close to Ridgway. My map showed that it ascended the pass, then descended to the Cimarron River and followed it north to US Highway 50 near Black Canyon of the Gunnison National Monument, where the Gunnison River has carved a spectacular sheer-walled canyon. Should be an interesting trip, I thought.

The weather was pleasant—hot, in fact—when I turned left just east of Ridgway

and followed the dusty road in its gradual climb. The views southwest across the Uncompahgre Valley toward snow-covered Mount Sneffels (14,150 feet in elevation) and other peaks of the San Juan Mountains were spectacular. Ahead were the rugged pinnacles of Courthouse Mountain.

Springtime in the Rockies is, indeed, something special. Take an ample quantity of solar energy, add a liberal dash of melting snow, top it off with a profusion of wild flowers, and you have some of the ingredients of its splendor.

Within a few miles of the main highway I began to realize that I was passing through a transition in seasons. The valley, as I said, was hot. It was early summer here—green meadows, cottonwoods in full leaf. As the road ascended, the scrub oaks were not only leafed out but beginning to look somewhat dry and dusty. Farther on, the quaking aspen were a deep green, the leaves fluttering in the slightest breeze. Soon I reached an elevation where the groves of aspen were just

153

beginning to be touched with a blush of spring green, a color that almost rivals autumn's gold in brilliance. Continuing on, I moved into an earlier and earlier spring landscape and soon the incipient aspen

leaves were tucked tightly into their pointed buds. There was evidence that the snow had been gone here only a short time. The grass was still dull brown and matted down. I did find one meadow with a southern exposure

154

that was green and filled with thousands of marsh marigolds, so I stopped here to relax and have lunch.

As the road continued its upward climb and turned through dark, thick forests of Engelmann spruce and Douglas fir, I began to notice patches of snow. Soon the road grew wet and muddy and the snow patches coalesced into a continuous white in the forest and along the road's edge. Very early

Near the turnoff for Owl Creek Pass

Mount Sneffels

spring. But I knew, of course, that once I started down the other side of the pass into the Cimarron River Valley I would soon be back to early summer.

Rounding a muddy curve, I found a thick patch of snow several yards long in my path, so I gunned the van and zipped across it, the back wheels spinning and sliding. I figured that I must be near the top of the pass, and I hoped that I'd soon begin descending into warmer climes.

Wrong. I wheeled around one last muddy bend and my excursion was over.

Ahead the road disappeared beneath an unbroken blanket of snow several feet thick. Winter.

I got out and explored on foot for a few hours, then retraced my path to camp for the night near the meadow full of marigolds. Next day I headed back down into the Uncompahgre Valley. Nothing wrong with seeing the same scenery twice when it's nice, but I made a promise to myself that I'd return to Owl Creek Pass sometime to see what the other side looks like. Soon I was back in summer again.

156

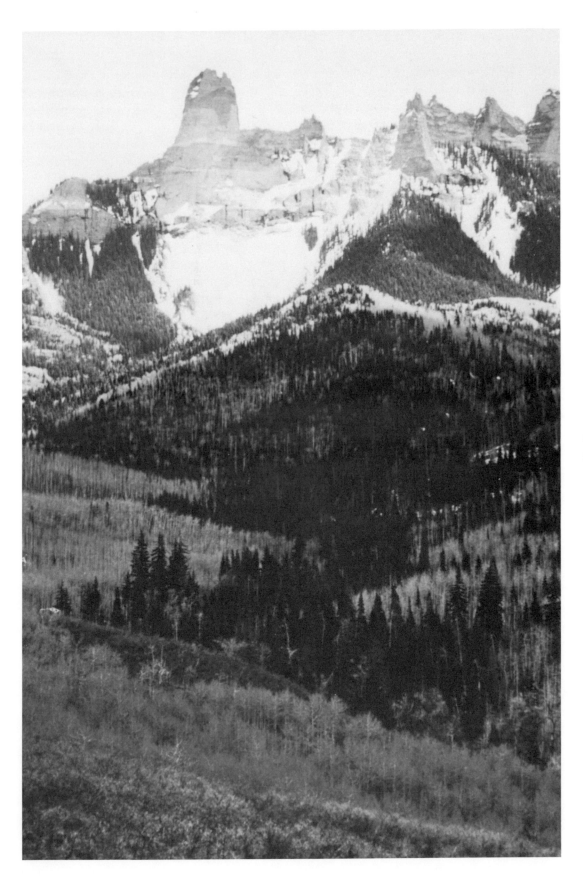

*Courthouse
Mountain*

RIDGWAY TO THE SAN MIGUEL VALLEY

THIS TOUR, which begins in Ridgway, is not a long one in distance covered, but it can occupy a day or two because it takes you down along the East Fork of the Dallas Creek, where you'll want to linger before doubling back to the main road.

About 25 miles south of Montrose, US Highway 550 runs into Colorado Highway 62, which heads west toward Dallas Divide. Less than a mile from the intersection is the town of Ridgway with many lovely old buildings dating from the area's boom days. (Incidentally, Ridgway and its environs will be inundated if the proposed Dallas Creek Dam is ever built.)

Six miles southwest of Ridgway turn left off Highway 62 and follow the US Forest Service signs to the Dallas Creek East Fork campground. As you're driving the several miles to the campground, you have a contin-

ual view of the ragged spires of Mount Sneffels towering above the aspen and pines that line the road. The campground isn't particularly large, but when I got there I had it to myself and spent the afternoon exploring on foot the meadows and aspen groves nearby.

Perhaps the most striking feature of this area, aside from Mount Sneffels looming overhead, is the creek itself. In fact, it's one of the most beautiful mountain streams I've ever come across. I spent hours hiking alongside it and photographing its numerous cascades. The creek winds and tumbles through a thick forest of Engelmann and blue spruce, adding to the charm of this place. In the summer delicate blossoms of red columbine wave along the rocky banks of the stream. Water ouzels nest in niches and alcoves mere inches from the roaring waters. These rather drab-looking birds—they are

BELOW: *Close-ups of buildings in Ridgway*

FACING PAGE: *Mount Wilson*

slate gray—are entertaining not only for their lovely song, but for their hunting antics as well. Perched on a convenient rock, they bob up and down while waiting for some insect larvae to come into view. Then they dive into the chill waters and submerge themselves for several seconds before emerging, perfectly dry, with their prey in their mouths.

From the campground there are trails that lead into the alpine country of the Mount Sneffels area. This range—and it is actually that rather than a single peak—has been proposed as a national wilderness to preserve its pristine beauty, and it certainly deserves such designation. Some of the lowland forests would be included in the boundaries of protection. And none too soon, for when you follow the road beyond the campground, you pass hillsides scarred from logging.

As the road continues, it twists and turns, gradually climbing, eventually becom-

ABOVE: *Mountains near Ridgway*

FACING PAGE: *Ruins in Hovenweep National Monument*

161

ing two dusty wheel ruts crossing a series of cattle guards. I pulled into an aspen grove and spent the afternoon lying in the hot sun in a marvelous meadow of wild flowers—eating a leisurely lunch and sipping wine while watching the clouds slip past the rugged peaks and planning some future hiking trips up into the mountains. And later, enjoying the play of sunset colors on the snowy top of Mount Sneffels. As I said, you'll want to linger.

When you return to Highway 62, turn left. As you continue west, the road climbs to the summit of Dallas Divide (elevation 8,970

feet). It is my personal opinion that the views along this stretch of Highway 62 are some of the finest in Colorado—especially in autumn. In the foreground are spruce and aspen forests, lovely ranches, and winding dirt roads lined with picturesque rail fences. To the south of course is the jagged outline of Mount Sneffels.

From Dallas Divide the road drops steeply, cutting down through the colorful canyon carved by Leopard Creek, a tributary of the San Miguel River, and it comes to an end at Placerville, where it meets Colorado Highway 145.

*View from
Dallas Divide*

TELLURIDE AND THE DOLORES RIVER

THE TRIP to Telluride begins at Placerville—presumably named for the placer deposits of gold once found in the region—on Colorado Highway 145. Northwest of Placerville this road winds through steep sandstone canyons of maroon-colored rock and leads to the little towns of Norwood, Redvale, and Naturita in the lovely San Miguel Valley. However, some of my favorite country, including Telluride and the Dolores River area, is reached by turning left. The road begins to climb, gradually at first, following the sparkling San Miguel River in a southeasterly direction. Soon it becomes steeper and as you leave the confines of the red rock canyon, you can see the San Miguel Mountains and the 14,017-foot pyramid of Wilson Peak to the south. Continuing on, you come to Telluride via a short spur road off the main highway.

If there is any place in Colorado that bears a resemblance to Switzerland or Austria, this is it. The town of Telluride sits in a u-shaped valley with mountains rising sharply on three sides. The name *Telluride,*

Mountains and barns near Telluride

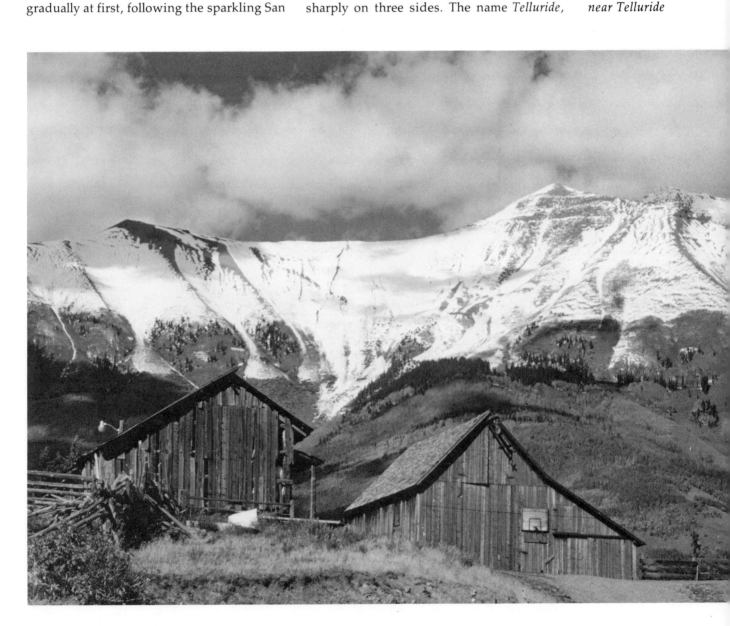

incidentally, is derived from the element tellurium, found here in conjunction with gold. The town was once one of the state's most active gold camps and is still known as "The City of Gold." Take time to wander up and down its main street to visit the hotel, city hall, and other late nineteenth-century buildings. The bank, built of large red sandstone blocks, is the one robbed by Butch Cassidy and his gang in 1889. The road continues past the town to a still-operating mine at Pandora, then winds in steep switchbacks up toward the magnificent 365-foot-high Bridal Veil Falls. Eventually the roadbed becomes rather rough and four-wheel drive is necessary.

RIGHT: *One of Telluride's old buildings*

FACING PAGE: *Bridal Veil Falls*

164

In the middle of Telluride begins another interesting side trip. Follow the signs pointing the way to Bear Creek Canyon. The road climbs through aspen groves and after a drive of only about one mile ends in a mountain-rimmed basin with another magnificent waterfall plunging into a pool.

South of the Telluride turnoff, Highway 145 continues to climb, up to and past the old boomtown of Ophir (named for the biblical location of King Solomon's mines), where it turns southwest. There are sensational views along this route of Mount Wilson and Wilson Peak in the San Miguel Mountains. Beyond Ophir, you come to Lizard Head Pass (elevation 10,222 feet) at the beginning

of the Dolores River drainage. From here the road drops down and follows the river as it swells in volume from its numerous tributaries. A few miles below the pass is the turnoff for Dunton and the West Dolores River, described next. Staying on Highway 145 you'll go through the town of Rico, with its scarred and denuded hillsides. Gold and silver were mined here in the 1870s, and Rico (Spanish for "rich") once boasted 6,000 inhabitants. The mining conducted in the area today is for lead, zinc, and copper. South of Rico the Dolores becomes a swift and sizable river, and you may see both kayakers and rafting parties challenging the fast waters.

*Headwaters of
the Dolores River at
Lizard Head Pass*

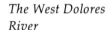

The West Dolores River

DUNTON

THE DRIVE to Dunton is short enough to be taken as an extension of the Telluride and Dolores River trip, described earlier. But this isn't your typical side excursion, for Dunton is a very special place. So special, in fact, that I include it here with great reluctance.

When you leave Telluride and head south on Colorado Highway 145, you begin the long climb to the top of Lizard Head Pass. As you start down the south side of the pass, keep a sharp eye out for an obscure road on the right and a sign reading DUN-TON. This road climbs sharply from Highway 145 and winds through a glorious grove

of aspen. It is a dirt road, rough in places, but passable for most cars. (I think I'd hesitate to attempt pulling a camping trailer or driving a low-slung car over it.)

After winding up over another small pass and down a forested hillside, the road parallels the West Dolores River. This lovely stream—it hardly appears to be a river at this point—meanders gently through open willow flats and spruce forests before joining the Dolores River west of Stoner. About eight miles from where you turned off Highway 145, you will arrive at the former gold-mining town of Dunton. But don't expect a

Cabin in Dunton

typical ghost town. This collection of old log buildings—a store, a saloon, some cabins, and a hotel—is now privately owned and operated as a resort—and a rather inexpensive one, I might add. Here you can soak away your cares in the delightful hot springs, housed in a decrepit old building (why worry about a leaking roof when you're immersed in a pool of 100-degree water?); fish in the clear waters of the West Dolores; or spend days just wandering in the densely forested mountains that surround the valley. Much of this land is soft and gentle, remind-

ing me of parts of New England. And the autumns here, like those in New England, are spectacular. A most magnificent place. Small wonder that Butch Cassidy and his gang made it a point to stop in Dunton after robbing the bank over in Telluride in 1889. That's right, you can sip a drink in the old saloon and rub elbows with the ghost of the infamous outlaw himself.

Oh, one other thing. Don't bother phoning ahead for reservations here at Dunton. You see, they still don't have any telephones in the area.

HOVENWEEP NATIONAL MONUMENT

ONE OF my favorite places in all of Colorado is Hovenweep National Monument, though only half of it is in the state. The other half is in Utah. Furthermore, the monument is not one single area, but consists of six scattered clusters of ruins—two in Utah and four in Colorado.

The best way to get there is from Cortez, in the southwest corner of Colorado. Here US Highway 666 heads northwest and eventually leads into Utah. Long before reaching the state line, however, and about 20 miles from Cortez, you pass through the little town of Pleasant View. Follow the signs here to the monument. The road runs straight west and then generally southwest.

This is arid country. It's also flat, open country with distant views of the mountains to the east. In the spring there is quite a contrast between the freshly plowed, brilliant red soil and the green of newly sprouted crops. Eventually you leave the last of the

169

irrigated farmland and travel through juniper and piñon forests with fragrant sagebrush growing in profusion.

About 23 miles from Pleasant View, and just inside Utah, you'll arrive at the small ranger station at the Square Tower Ruins, the largest and best preserved of the six units and the most accessible. Before doing any exploring, you should go inside to learn the significance of this place. There's a campground nearby, but you'll have to bring your own equipment.

Hovenweep was the home of a pre-Columbian Indian people believed to be the ancestors of the modern-day Pueblos. They were related to, and perhaps even traded with, the residents of Mesa Verde some 30 miles to the southeast. Unlike the Mesa Verde people, however, the inhabitants of Hovenweep did not enjoy the security of massive cliff dwellings; the flatness of the land here is broken only by shallow canyons carved into the buff-colored sandstone. Instead, these people had to build smaller

The Cliff Palace, Mesa Verde National Park

171

structures from flat rocks on the edges of canyons and gullies.

To me the appeal of Hovenweep is the sense of history and tragedy it imparts. It is almost never crowded, and you can wander about by yourself, find your own private ruin, and sit quietly listening to the ghosts of a distant past. Naturally, you are expected to leave things as they are, and souvenir collecting is strictly prohibited.

The area was first inhabited around the time of the birth of Christ by nomads in search of small game and forage who built small, temporary shelters of wooden poles and mud. Later, from about 900 AD to 1200 AD these people constructed more solid, permanent structures of rock, which offered some protection against hostile intruders. They also began to grow crops to alleviate their dependence on far-ranging and sparse game as their food staple.

The Indians survived quite well in this harsh land until about 1276 AD (a date established by tree ring dating). That year marked the onset of a 23-year drought that eventually—along with internal disagreements and invasions by outside groups—forced the inhabitants of Mesa Verde, Hovenweep, and other places to leave their ancestral lands and migrate south to wetter regions in the Rio Grande and Gila River valleys. The people never returned, and the ruins of their dwellings stand as a sad and silent monument to a natural disaster.

In visiting Hovenweep, allow plenty of time to roam about the clusters of ruins and the canyons. It seems a harsh, barren place at first, but there are touches of beauty to be found, especially in May and June, when the desert flowers are in bloom.

Incidentally, even though you won't find them on your map, there are roads leading to all the ruins. But except for the one which took you to the ranger station, they are dirt roads that may be washed out in bad weather.

To return to Cortez and to the vicinity of Mesa Verde National Park for a highly recommended side trip, follow the McElmo Canyon road back east to US 666 and then head north a few miles to Cortez. About nine miles east of Cortez on US Highway 160 is the entrance to the park (16 miles south of here is the Visitor Center). Mesa Verde is much larger, and more crowded than Hovenweep, and you are allowed to visit the cliff dwellings only on Park Service guided tours. But even though a drive to the park hardly qualifies as an adventuresome backroad trip, you shouldn't pass it up, for the Mesa Verde ruins are even more impressive than those at Hovenweep.

The Great Plains

Wᴇ ALL SEEM TO HAVE PREFERENCES FOR—or perhaps prejudices against— certain landforms. There are the desert rats, who love nothing better than the sun-seared land of sand, cactus, and slickrock. Mountain folks never quite seem comfortable away from their rocky ramparts, deep winter snows, and color-splashed summer tundra. For others the pounding, moody seacoasts are home. And then there are the flatlanders, who like their land uncluttered, free and open, where the vast expanse of sky can be scrutinized for clues of the day-after-tomorrow's weather. For those who love mountains or for whom deserts have a quickly grasped charm, the prairies are definitely an acquired taste. But it's not hard to learn to love this land, or at least to appreciate it. Perhaps Willa Cather—in *Death Comes for the Archbishop*—best describes the character of the flatlands:

Elsewhere the sky is the roof of the world; but here the earth was the floor of the sky. The landscape one longed for when one was far away, the thing all about one, the world one actually lived in, was the sky, the sky!

Mention Colorado, and most people think of mountains. Yet more than a third of the state lies in the domain of the Great Plains, that vast sweep of prairie extending eastward from the Rockies to the Mississippi. In many ways this flatland of eastern Colorado has more of an Old West flavor than the High Country. This is the land of the Plains Indian—the Pawnee, the Cheyenne, the Comanche, the Arapaho. It's still possible here to sense the expansiveness that awed the mountain men, the members of the Pike and Long expeditions, the gold seekers, and the immigrant settlers. This is Kit Carson country, former home of the bison, cattle barons, and sodbusters, rich in history, tinged with irony, marked with tragedy. Earth, sky, grass, cactus, yucca all come together here. Short-grass prairie, tall-grass prairie. A land where much of the original prairie has been tamed, changed to farming and ranching country with irrigation, and where oil wells sprout amid the crops and browsing cattle.

For a land that seems so stark and barren—it was once called the "great American desert"—it can be rich and fecund. Gentle springs with yellow cactus blossoms, creamy yucca flowers, new-green grass, and the smell of sweet damp earth. Amber autumns, the mellow season of waving grass and grain and the sounds of geese and ducks heading south once more. There are more than 150 species of birds, ranging from prairie falcon and golden eagle to sandhill crane, meadowlark, and blackcapped chickadee. The bison are gone, at least the immense numbers of them that once roamed here, but the pronghorn antelope, once near extinction, are thriving. From rattlesnake to prairie dog, many of the original inhabitants are still here.

Because it is a more subtle land, traveling the backroads of the Great Plains requires time—time, that is, to stop and roam a bit to see, smell, and hear the prairie. In some places a sense of historical perspective can be realized only by leaving car and road far behind and out of sight. But sometimes it's necessary to wander only a short distance to absorb the essence of the prairie, to learn what it's all about.

Like the Western Slopes, this section of the state usually enjoys early springs and late autumns. But for a terrain so simple, the weather in the Great Plains can have its violent aspects. Although summer storms are severe enough in the High Country, they sometimes have a special ferocity in the flatlands. Hot searing summers, with afternoon thunderstorms moving across the open lands in ponderous, billowing black clouds, blasting rains into the parched soil with ear-shattering, heart-pounding thunder and lightning. Cold winters, with biting winds and drifting snows. And though they may be rare in the mountains, tornadoes are not at all uncommon in eastern Colorado.

In traveling the backroads of the plains, it's best to keep an eye on the weather. Fortunately the uncluttered view while you're driving makes this easy, giving you ample warning of approaching storms—sometimes hours before they hit. It's a good idea also to listen to a local station on the car radio if the impending storm looks particularly ominous, for tornado

*Windmill
near Fondis*

warnings may be given under these conditions. Regardless of the estimated severity of the forecast, you may want to think about heading back to a main highway. Even the briefest of thunderstorms can transform a dusty backroad into an impassable quagmire. I spent one very long afternoon out near the Pawnee Buttes trying to drive a rain-soaked road. My Dodge van may be a marvelous machine, but it was pushed to its limits that day in axle-deep mud.

Unlike the High Country, much of the land in this part of the state is privately owned, the exception being the Pawnee and Comanche national grasslands (under the jurisdiction of the US Forest Service, in case you want more information). Fences and roads of farms and ranches should be respected. It is usually possible to obtain permission from farmers and ranchers to roam about on some of their land, and while you're conversing with them, you'll often hear fascinating stories of local history. These are a people proud of their land, with a strong sense of appreciation for its subtle beauty.

Plains Indian encampment along the South Platte River south of present-day Greeley

177

PAWNEE NATIONAL GRASSLAND

THIS TRIP begins at Ault, on Colorado Highway 14 about ten miles north of Greeley. The road heads east through rolling, gentle farm country, then enters Pawnee National Grassland, a 772,000-acre area of low, grass-covered hills and sandstone buttes. At first there seems to be little difference between the farmland around Ault and the grassland, but soon it's obvious that this is uncultivated and unirrigated country, for it's much drier than the lush wheat fields to the west.

In the 1930s, the US government bought the farms and ranches from the homesteaders who wanted to leave the dust bowl, and then began reseeding the purchased land so it would once again have a protective covering of grass. The people who wanted to stay on here were encouraged to convert to cattle ranching. Today, as a result

of the government program, most of Pawnee National Grassland is covered by blue grama and buffalo grass, the short prairie grasses native to the region. Over half of the area is still privately owned, but the land is now being used primarily for grazing sheep and cattle.

The grassland is ornithologist Roger Tory Peterson's favorite place in all of Colorado, and it didn't take me long to discover why. The blue grama and buffalo grass support a huge bird population. I saw mountain plovers, prairie falcons, and Swainson's hawks, to name a few, and you can expect to see countless other species. (According to the US Department of Agriculture, at least 225 different species of birds have been sighted here since 1962.)

About midway between Ault and Sterling, I turned north on a gravel road and followed signs to Keota. This once-thriving community is now a virtual ghost town. Only one of the dozen houses seemed to be inhabited, and the dry wind blew tumbleweeds down the deserted street. (It's ironically appropriate that the name *Keota* is derived from an Indian word meaning "gone to visit.")

From here I followed numerous dirt roads north and east to different parts of the Pawnee Buttes, the sandstone and chalk cliffs that rise above the rest of the grassland. The buttes were among the first places in Colorado to be studied by paleontologists, and many fossils of plains animals have been found in the sandstone strata.

This is country to explore on foot. I wandered up sandy draws, smelling the sweet-pungent aroma of sagebrush and looking for yellow cactus blossoms. The landscape was dotted with swordlike yucca plants, and in one of those dry creek beds I came upon a beautiful bull snake.

In the walls of the buttes are many caves and alcoves. I enjoyed sitting here alone, imagining Cheyenne or Arapaho lookouts watching for bison or enemy tribes from this same spot. And way, way on the distant horizon I could see the shimmering snow of Longs Peak.

The Pawnee Buttes

*Pawnee National
Grassland*

Few of the roads north of Keota are marked, but that makes taking them much more of an adventure. There's little danger of getting lost, for you can always backtrack. On one of these obscure lanes I came over a rise to surprise a small herd of pronghorn antelope. They raced along in front of the van, and I clocked them at 35 miles per hour before they veered off toward the foothills.

My blunderings eventually took me to New Raymer and Highway 14 again, then on to Sterling.

ALONG THE SOUTH PLATTE RIVER

WHEN I left Sterling, turning right on US Highway 6, I expected the jaunt southeast along the South Platte River to be quick and uneventful. Though the trip looks short on the map (it's only about 20 miles), you can spend a lot of time poking around the bottomlands, as I did. The road is quieter than you would expect, for US 6, once the main highway from Denver to Sterling to Nebraska and points east, has been supplanted in Colorado by Interstate 76—one of those cases where a main highway has now become a backroad.

The name *Platte* was bestowed on the river by some early French trappers, who called it *Rivière la Platte*, meaning "shallow river" or "thin river." And shallow it is. In fact, the stream is broken into numerous channels and sloughs, each of them shallow enough to wade.

There is a strong sense of history along this stretch of the river. Perhaps a few of the magnificent old cottonwoods in the area were saplings when Kit Carson, Bill Williams, and other fur trappers followed the South Platte toward old Fort Vasquez between present-day Denver and Greeley in the 1830s. Seven miles south of Sterling, just

180

east of US 6 on Colorado Highway 63, a state historical marker directs you to a monument on the site of the Summit Springs battleground. At the springs, southeast of here, the US cavalry and 150 Pawnee scouts, guided by Buffalo Bill Cody, surprised and overwhelmed the Cheyenne in the last (July 1869) Plains Indian battle fought in the state. Chief Tall Bull and his "Dog Soldiers" had been raiding Kansas and Colorado settlements. Where US 6 crosses over to the south bank of the river, another tablet marks the site of Old Fort Wicked. This Overland Stage station and stockade was the only one in the South Platte area to survive the Indian attacks during a rampage along a 100-mile stretch. The station master, H. Godfrey, put up such a good fight that the Indians nicknamed him "Old Wicked."

On the south side of the river, US 6 leads to Prewitt Reservoir. Along the western shore of the reservoir, set amid more lovely old cottonwoods, there's an excellent campground. For the evening's entertainment I watched a flock of white pelicans skimming the water and swooping in precision aerial acrobatics. The bird life here is astounding. Besides the pelicans, I spotted meadowlarks, ospreys, great blue herons, and several species of ducks.

Prewitt Reservoir

Colorado Sketch: THE MOUNTAIN MEN

IN A GREAT many ways the fur trappers and traders collectively known as the mountain men were a tougher, lustier breed than the miners or prospectors who followed them several decades later. Some of their names have become legend: Jim Bridger, Jedediah Smith, Kit Carson, Jim Beckwourth.

The two decades from 1820 to 1840 represented the golden era of the mountain men. It was a whim of fashion in Europe and the Eastern United States—beaver hats—that created a demand for their skills, though other furs were also popular. Roaming far and wide throughout the Rocky Mountain area and beyond, they trapped beavers and sold the pelts at annual summer rendezvous, where they combined business with all-round hell-raising. Some were loners—"free trappers." Others worked for such companies as John Jacob Astor's American Fur Company (known simply as "The Company"), the Rocky Mountain Fur Company (owned for a while by Jedediah Smith, William L. Sublette, and David E. Jackson, for whom Jackson Hole, in Wyoming, is named), the Hudson's Bay Company, or General William H. Ashley's firm. Ashley employed about 300 men in the West.

It was with Ashley that Jedediah Smith, probably the greatest mountain man of them all, got his start. Unlike most of the fur trappers, Smith was a well-educated and religious man, who toted a Bible and a volume of Shakespeare's plays in his pack. Other Ashley employees were Beckwourth and the legendary Mike Fink. During a rendezvous, Fink killed his buddy in a shooting match. He claimed it was an accident—they were both drunk—but he must not have been very convincing, for to this day many people think his name is the origin for the word meaning treacherous or contemptible. Later Fink himself met a violent death while on one of Ashley's fur-trapping expeditions. Beckwourth, the son of a Virginia planter and a black slave, gave up trapping to live with the Crow Indians, eventually becoming a war chief. He had convinced them he was one of them, that he'd been kidnapped as a child.

It was a dangerous way of life. The trappers lived off the land and at times the land was unforgiving of mistakes in judgment. More than a few of them died of starvation, froze to death, or drowned in a raging river. Grizzly bears, plentiful inhabitants of the Rockies then, killed or maimed others. At this time the Rocky Mountain West was still largely *terra incognita*, the only knowledge of the terrain provided by the expeditions led by Meriwether Lewis and William Clark in 1804-06, and by Zebulon Pike and Stephen H. Long in 1806 and 1820 respectively.

The mountain men, in their extensive wanderings, discovered many of the natural wonders of the West long before they were "rediscovered" decades later by government expeditions. When John Colter, who left the Lewis and Clark Expedition to go into fur trapping, described the geysers and hot springs in what is now Yellowstone National Park—he is credited with being the first white man to see them—no one believed him. "Colter's Hell," his "hallucinations" were called. Nor did Jim Bridger fare any better a little later. His descriptions of the same area were dubbed "Bridger's lies."

Not only was the wilderness itself an adversary, but certain Indian tribes, the Blackfeet in particular, were hostile and brutal in their dealings with the trappers. Many mountain men lost their lives and scalps at the hands of the Indians.

Was it worth the danger? Did they earn enough money to compensate for such perils and privations? While potential wealth may have been their initial incentive, history has shown that few of the trappers made much money from their dangerous ventures. The real fortunes were made by the owners of the fur companies, by such men as John Jacob Astor in their towers of Eastern commerce. For the mountain men, however, there were other rewards. Warren Angus Ferris was employed by Astor's American Fur Company in 1830. He kept meticulous journals of his adventures and in one made this observation:

The very danger has its attraction, and the courage and cunning, and skill, and watchfulness made necessary by the difficulties they [the mountain men] have to overcome, the privations they are forced to contend with, and the perils against which they must guard, become at once their pride and boast. A strange, wild, terrible, romantic, hard, and exciting life they lead, with alternate plenty and starvation, activity and repose, safety and alarm, and all the other adjuncts that belong to so vagrant a condition in a harsh, barren, untamed, and fearful region of desert, plain and mountain. Yet so attached to it do they become that few ever leave it. . . .

Some mountain men were inveterate wanderers. Crossing country that had never been explored by white men before, Jedediah Smith twice trekked to California and back, the second journey so perilous that it cost the lives of most of his companions. After a final, highly profitable fur-trapping expedition, he tried to quit but couldn't. While leading a wagon train to Santa Fe in 1831—a job he had volunteered for—the great trailblazer was ambushed by a band of Comanches and killed, but not before the redoubtable Smith had dispatched several of his attackers.

By the early 1840s heavy trapping had almost exterminated the beaver. Meanwhile, more permanent fur-trading establishments had been built in Colorado. Fort Vasquez, constructed in 1837 by Louis Vasquez and Andrew Sublette near present-day Denver, was one of these. More important was Bent's Old Fort, completed in 1833, on the north bank of the Arkansas River (described later).

The declining years of the fur trade overlapped the westward migration of settlers and gold seekers. Bent's Fort was fortuitously located on the Santa Fe Trail and became an important stopping point for travelers and for traders handling goods of every description. Former mountain men such as Kit Carson became scouts. Carson guided three of John Charles Frémont's expeditions across Colorado in the 1840s. During the Civil War he served in the Union Army, rising to the brevet rank of brigadier general.

The era of the mountain men was one of the most colorful in Rocky Mountain history. In his book, *Across the Wide Missouri,* Bernard DeVoto describes the excitement and danger of their way of life:

The mountain men were a tough race, as many selective breeds of Americans have had to be; their courage, skill, and mastery of the conditions of their chosen life were absolute or they would not have been here. Nor would they have been here if they had not responded to the loveliness of the country and found . . . something precious beyond safety, gain, comfort, and family life.

GREELEY TO DEARFIELD

THE TOWN of Greeley, at the juncture of US highways 85 and 34, has an interesting history. In 1869 a group of people gathered at the Cooper Institute in New York to hear Horace Greeley, owner of the *New York Trib-une*, talk about forming a cooperative farming community, to be called Union Colony, in Colorado. Before the evening was over several memberships at 15 dollars each had been sold. The only two stipulations were that a member had to be of good moral character and had to abstain from drinking any alcoholic beverage.

Though it was named for Greeley, the town was founded by the *Tribune*'s agricultural editor, Nathan C. Meeker, in 1870.

*Greeley in
the 1920s*

When Isabella Bird visited the community three years later, it had 3,000 inhabitants. She called it "the most prosperous and rising colony in Colorado," but complained that it was hot and full of bugs. This could explain why Horace Greeley visited the town but never lived there. Meeker's home is now a museum, preserving many of his effects and other historical mementos. Incidentally, there is a Colorado town named after Meeker, along the White River (described earlier). He's the Indian agent killed in the Ute uprising (the "Meeker Massacre") when he headed the White River Agency.

From Greeley turn east on US 34, a long stretch of which roughly parallels the South Platte. Where the river makes a loop south and then north of the road, look for a highway sign indicating the site of Dearfield, another farming commune.

185

This cooperative farming venture was started by O. T. Jackson and a tiny band of followers in 1910. It became successful, the new farmers learning as they went about such things as soil conservation and dry farming. Around 1920, the community of Dearfield (so named because the fields had become dear to the inhabitants) could boast a population of 700. By 1929, it was being advertised as a resort—with a lodge, dance pavilion, lunchroom, filling station, with lakes nearby as well as proximity (only 70 miles) to Denver.

Then came the depression and the drought and dust storms of the 1930s. By 1940, the community had dwindled to 12 people. The founder finally gave up too and moved back to Denver, where he died in 1949. Dearfield became a ghost town.

Dearfield's story is much more typical of communes in Colorado than is Greeley's. But there's one thing that sets it apart from the others. Dearfield was settled by and for blacks.

Today there's a working gas station here. The ruins of the lunchroom and several old houses are still to be seen. They're all that remain of one black man's dream of making it in a white society.

For a pleasant side trip from Dearfield, especially if the day is hot, it's a short drive to the Jackson Lake Reservoir State Park. About six miles east of Dearfield, Colorado Highway 39 heads north to Goodrich, from which a well-marked paved road leads to the park.

I was surprised to see cars hauling boats, seemingly so out of place on the flat, dry plains. I found out why when I came to the reservoir—it covers 2,000 acres. Besides boating, the park offers swimming, picnicking, and camping. A special pass, which can be bought at the gate, is required and a small fee is charged for camping.

BRUSH TO LIMON

Cattle and antelope along Colorado Highway 71

COLORADO Highway 71 between Brush and Limon is a quick way to get from the Pawnee Grassland area to central and southeastern Colorado. The highway runs through the heartland of Colorado's farming region, past spacious cattle ranches and irrigated fields of sugar beets and wheat. Interestingly enough, I saw quite a variety of wildlife along this road. First there were the birds: meadowlarks, magpies, ravens, three golden

8 mi.

N

River

Platte

South

25

76

Box Elder Cr.

BRUSH

71

LAST
CHANCE

36

70

71

DENVER

83

Cherry Cr.

FRANKTOWN

CASTLE
ROCK

ELIZABETH

KIOWA

Running Cr.

86

LIMON

25

83

■

ELBERT

FONDIS

Running Cr.
Field
Station

Black
Forest

To
Colorado
Springs
8 miles

The Last Chance Cafe

eagles, a couple of prairie falcons, and—almost every quarter of a mile—a beautiful little sparrow hawk perched on a fence post watching for an unwary field mouse. Then there were those crazy antelope all over the place, mingling and grazing contentedly with the Herefords and Angus. I also spotted a badger and a couple of deer down in a draw next to the road.

The gentle, rolling country caused me to think about what this land was like when it was inhabited by the Indians. There was a time when the plains thundered with the hooves of buffalo, or American bison. Estimates place the number of these shaggy beasts at about 30 million in the region east of the Rockies before the white man arrived.

Here in eastern Colorado the Plains Indians—Arapaho, Cheyenne, Comanche, and others—were strongly dependent on the buffalo, not only as their major source of food, but also for their clothing, shelter, tools, and weapons. It was the wholesale slaughter by white men that diminished the herds. First gold, then free land brought large numbers of immigrants to the West. The huge buffalo herds must have seemed an infinite resource, for they were hunted with incredible waste. "Sportsmen" journeyed to the plains solely for the pleasure of killing immense numbers of the animals and often left the carcasses to rot. By 1887 these once plentiful animals had virtually disappeared. Today, except for certain small, preserved herds, the buffalo are gone from the area.

If you're near Brush early in July, you might want to take in the world's largest amateur rodeo, part of a three-day festival ending on the Fourth.

The road took me through the village of Last Chance, so named because it was once the last gasoline stop between here and the Denver area (I'm sorry I inquired—I'd hoped for a more intriguing explanation), and on through pleasant country with many nicely kept farms and ranches. Limon, founded in 1888 as a railroad camp, is still very much a railroad town, situated at the juncture of the Union Pacific and the Chicago, Rock Island & Pacific lines.

CASTLE ROCK AND "BEAUTIFUL DOWNTOWN ELBERT"

IT IS generally assumed that the Great Plains section of the state is flat, featureless, and except for small cottonwood groves here and there along stream courses, also devoid of forests. So this loop trip, from Castle Rock and back to Franktown, might possibly be the most surprising of all the backroad tours in Colorado, for it encompasses a different kind of terrain in the "flatlands"—the northern extension of the Black Forest country. The Black Forest is a unique ecological feature located between Colorado Springs and Denver, and east of the Front Range and Rampart Range. Basically it is a high, rolling tableland, a transition zone between mountains and plains. Extensive forests of ponderosa pine and lush meadows cover these hills. Intermingled with the grasses are cactus and yucca, typical dry-land vegetation. The average elevation is 6,000 feet above sea level, and the most deceptive feature of the area is its very gradual rise to almost 7,500 feet—higher than my home in Evergreen up in the Front Range. Small but lovely canyons have been carved by such streams as Cherry Creek and Running Creek as they flow northward to join the South Platte River.

The trip begins at Castle Rock on Colorado Highway 86, just off Interstate 25, about 25 miles south of Denver. The town's name is derived from a prominent local rock formation and was first coined by the Major Stephen H. Long expedition in 1820. The

A backroad near Elbert

courthouse here is one of those marvelous old structures built of massive sandstone blocks and intended to last for a millennium or two.

I followed Highway 86 east from Castle Rock through Franktown, Elizabeth, and Kiowa. To me this drive is reminiscent of the Mogollon Rim country in northern Arizona, with its stately, dark ponderosa forests interspersed with grassy meadows. Pikes Peak looms massive and snowy to the southwest. The farther east you travel on this road, the more rural it becomes.

At Kiowa I headed south on a county road toward Elbert. An old mountain friend from Evergreen had moved here a few years before, and I was curious about the attraction, having kidded him about life in "beautiful downtown Elbert" before he left. I soon discovered its appeal. The town and the farms and ranches have a charm, character, and quietness difficult to find elsewhere in Colorado. There are no tourists here, and urban sprawl hasn't yet made an encroachment. I wandered around backroads in the area, past ranches tucked into verdant folds of land surrounded by stately forests. The view of the mountains to the west was inspiring.

A little place dot on my map, denoted as Fondis, is now a virtual ghost town. There are echos of better times though: an old general store with a rusting pump for dispensing kerosene, an abandoned cheese factory, and an old church.

From Elbert, I headed back west on an undesignated gravel road, passing an abandoned one-room schoolhouse along the way. About six miles west of the town is the Running Creek Field Station, an ecological learning center unique in the nation. Established by Elizabeth Wright Ingraham, granddaughter of Frank Lloyd Wright, the 960-acre center includes a preserve of mixed-grass prairie and a working farm. A canyon, formed by Running Creek, runs through the property. Each summer, students and scientists participate in seminars and research programs here. The field station is usually open on Sundays. But don't expect to drive through the complex. To view the unusual tetrahedral and triangular wood and canvas facilities designed by the sculptor Robert Behrens, for instance, you must leave your car at the entrance and hike more than a mile on a well-marked trail across rolling, flower-dotted prairie.

The final leg of the trip is on Colorado Highway 83 back north to Franktown, crossing the steep little gorge carved in sandstone by Cherry Creek. The diversity and beauty of this area should give even the most hardened skeptic and lover of high country a new appreciation of "them flatlands."

FACING PAGE:
*Roman Catholic
church in Elbert*

BIG SANDY CREEK

WHEN I turned off Colorado Highway 71 at Limon and drove southeast on US 287, I knew where I was heading. My destination was the site of the infamous Sand Creek Massacre, on Big Sandy Creek. What I didn't expect when I got there was the powerful impact this place would have on me.

At the town of Kit Carson the road turns right and south to Eads. Heading east from here, I looked for signs pointing the way to the massacre site. There were none. A couple of miles east of Chivington I spotted a stone historical marker indicating that the tragedy had taken place about 12 miles north of this spot, so I wheeled off the highway and followed the gravel road in that direction. Fortunately a few small signs had been erected near the site of the battle, for otherwise I might have spent several hours bouncing over the myriad dusty roads in the area.

I think it is fortunate that you can't drive directly to Big Sandy Creek. Instead, you must park on a sand hill, where there's another small marker, and walk a quarter of a mile or so down into the little valley. The vulnerability of the camp's location among those old cottonwoods is very apparent as you amble down from the rise of land where the US Army troops launched their attack.

What *did* happen here? On the morning of November 29, 1864, Colonel John Chivington and several hundred of his men mounted a surprise attack on the combined Arapaho and Cheyenne encampment along Big Sandy Creek. Expecting hundreds of armed warriors, Chivington discovered mainly old men, women, and children among the 600 Indians camped here. Nonetheless, the slaughter took place. When it was over, 105 women and children and 28 men in the camp lay dead, while nine of Chivington's soldiers died. The brutality was compounded when many of the Indian dead were scalped and some mutilated.

Today, Big Sandy Creek is an intermittent little stream, as it undoubtedly was then, flowing quietly through rolling sand country. The plains are quite dry here, almost desert. Along the creek bottom are immense cottonwoods. It is a lovely spot, but I had a decided feeling of tragedy, a sense of malevolent history as I wandered around. I spent a long time sitting among the trees, roaming up and down the stream, listening to the breeze stir the cottonwood leaves. The June sun was hot and it was a pleasant day, but I decided to leave rather than camp. There were just too many troubled spirits here. A sad piece of history for Colorado and the nation.

Along Big Sandy Creek

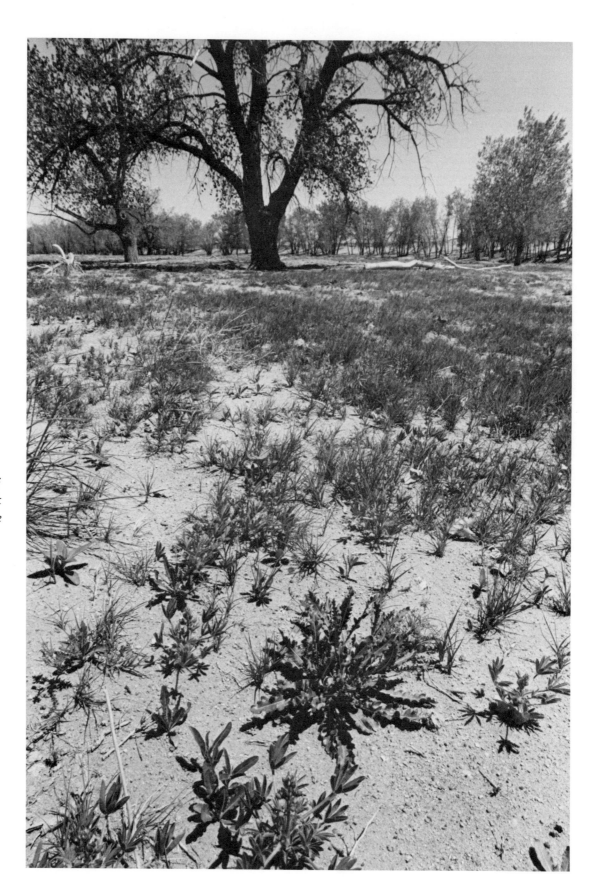

*Site of
the Sand Creek
Massacre*

*Sketch of
Bent's Fort
in 1845*

BENT'S OLD FORT

A GOOD place to begin this tour to Bent's Old Fort is at Lamar, a small town at the juncture of US Highway 50 and US 287. On Main Street is the Madonna of the Trail monument, a statue memorializing the pioneer mothers whose sacrifices made possible the settling of the West.

Leaving Lamar, first head north for a short distance, and then west, on US 50, which parallels the Arkansas River. At Hasty turn south onto an unmarked road that crosses the river and leads to the John Martin Reservoir. This access road runs between the

645,500-acre reservoir, the largest in Colorado, and man-made Lake Hasty. There's a first-rate campground near the recreational lake, where you can fish or just relax and enjoy the view.

Retrace your way back to US 50—it's a short drive—and continue west past Fort Lyon, a Veterans Administration Hospital; on the grounds is the cabin where Kit Carson lived and died and which now serves as a chapel. A few miles farther west, at the intersection of Colorado Highway 194 and US 50, turn south to Las Animas, worth a visit to

195

browse through the Kit Carson Museum with its many exhibits, including mementos of the famed scout. The pioneer jail and rural schoolhouse are part of the museum. William Bent is buried in the town cemetery. Double back the mile or so north to Highway 194, and about ten miles west of the turnoff, you'll come to Bent's Old Fort.

Charles and William Bent and their partner, Ceran St. Vrain, made a smart decision when they chose the northern banks of the Arkansas River, near present-day La Junta, as the site for their fort and trading post. The Mountain Branch of the Santa Fe Trail ran along the river through western Kansas and eastern Colorado, then veered southwest—at the spot where the fort was built—to enter New Mexico over Raton Pass. In the early 1820s, US merchants had become interested in trading with Mexico, which then controlled New Mexico. The land along the Arkansas River was the domain of the Plains Indians, who roamed far and wide in pursuit of buffalo, and of the mountain men, those hardy fur trappers who followed the Arkansas and South Platte rivers to the Rockies. Thus the fort was accessible to traders, Indians, and fur trappers alike.

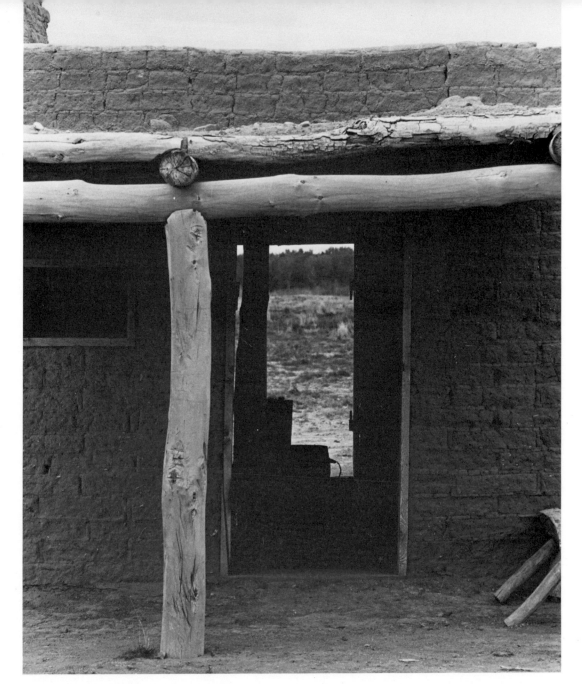

Bent's Fort was completed in 1833, though the huge structure was in use for some time before this. For 16 years it was the largest and most important trading center in the Southwest. It was an ideal place of exchange for goods being transported east and west: cloth, ammunition, beads, and supplies, shipped from the Mississippi Valley; buffalo robes, beaver pelts, silver, horses, and blankets, shipped east. It was also a natural stopover for those following the Santa Fe Trail and a popular social center for Indians, plainsmen, mountain men, and traders. Before the fort was abandoned and partially demolished in 1849, many of the heroes of the Old West—Jim Bridger, Jim (Medicine Calf) Beckwourth, R. L. ("Uncle Dick") Wootton, Kit Carson, and John C. Frémont, among others—either worked or passed through here.

Under the auspices of the National Park Service, the old adobe fort has been reconstructed on its original site, and it makes a fascinating place to visit, even if you're not a history buff. As you approach this imposing structure from the east, you'll understand

197

why more than one frontier traveler likened it to a medieval castle. Its 14-foot-high walls, twin round towers, and square watchtower give it the appearance of impregnability, an impression that is heightened when you pass through its tunnel-like entrance.

Allow plenty of time to explore the inside of the fort, for there is a great deal to see. The entire area enclosed by the outer walls is larger than a football field. As soon as you pass through the entranceway, you'll notice a square of rooms, each facing an inner courtyard. In the well-marked information center on the ground floor of the quadrangle you can obtain a map of the structure and a brochure explaining its extraordinary history. Most of the fort's 33 rooms have been furnished with antiques or reproductions of antique furniture from the 1830s. And if you plan your trip for the summer months, you'll be able to see "living history" demonstrations of frontier cooking, carpentry, and blacksmithing.

When you've finished touring the huge complex, you can mosey down to the Arkansas and listen to the music of flowing water. Chances are you'll find yourself lost in thought, ruminating as I did, on the colorful and tragic lives of Charles Bent, who conceived the idea of the fort, and his brother William, who managed and destroyed it (described next).

Colorado Sketch: THE BENTS AND THEIR FORT

GONE. They're all dead and gone, William Bent thought as he walked through the empty rooms of the fort. Three brothers. A wife. Half the southern Cheyenne—his friends.

William stooped to pick up a broken teacup from a pile of rubble. He remembered when it had arrived from St. Louis. An attempt to bring civilization to the wild frontier. He laughed remembering how the mountain men and Indians had teased him about becoming soft.

Maybe he had. He sure wasn't as tough as he had been in the 1820s when he started working with his brother Charles. You had to be tough to survive in those early days of the fur-trading business, what with the Indian attacks, blizzards, and starvation. Of course, that was many years ago, when he was only a kid. Now, in 1849, he was 40 years old.

There had been a lot of changes out here in the West during that time. He'd even been responsible for a few changes himself. This fort, for instance.

When he, Charles, and Ceran St. Vrain had formed their company, there was no trading post or fort on the Santa Fe Trail. The freighters loaded their wagons in Missouri and made a beeline for Santa Fe or Taos—hoping they would make it. They were at the mercy of the weather and Indians alike.

The fort had been Charles's idea. "Think what we could do with a post along the route," he'd said. "We could use it for protection and storage, and the Indians could come to us to trade their buffalo robes. And that's where the money's going to be in the future—buffalo robes, not beaver skins."

Yes, Charles had been the planner. But he, William, was the builder. Adobe was the logical building material, he'd decided, because for one thing it was fireproof and besides there wasn't enough timber available on the treeless plains for the sprawling fortress he had in mind. With 100 or so Mexican laborers working for him, it had taken a couple of years before the structure was completed.

William ran his hand over the smooth adobe wall. He remembered the day he'd ridden a couple of miles out onto the prairie, then turned around to look at the almost-completed building. Why, it looks like one of those huge old castles, right out of England or France or maybe

Spain, he'd thought. And he recalled how enormously pleased he had been.

So had Charles. "It's to be called William's Fort," he declared, but the name hadn't stuck. The mountain men called it Bent's Fort, so Bent's Fort it was. Which was only right, William reflected. Sure, he was the resident manager, but his brothers Robert and George had also worked hard to make the trading company a success.

And it had been a success. With me managing the fort, and Charles and St. Vrain taking care of the business end at Taos and Santa Fe, our firm had become the biggest trading company in the area served by the Santa Fe Trail.

You know, I wasn't a bad manager, William decided. It hadn't been easy, handling mountain men, Indians, soldiers, emigrants, and other assorted travelers who stopped at the fort.

He felt especially proud that the Indians had trusted him. I was fair with them, he thought, that's why. I was fair with them, I understood them, and I liked them. No, I loved them. Especially the Cheyenne.

Especially Owl Woman. She'd been so beautiful when he'd married her. She'd given him three children, then died when the fourth was born.

Stop it! William said to himself. Stop this confounded remembering! That part of my life is over, and the dead won't come back. Not Owl Woman. Not Robert, killed by a Comanche. Not George, dead of disease. Not all my Cheyenne friends, killed by the cholera epidemic brought by the emigrants. Not even Charles.

Charles. More father than older brother. Killed in Taos by a screaming mob of Mexicans and Indians, while his wife and children watched.

The good old US Army was to blame, William thought bitterly. If the government hadn't started the war with Mexico and sent the army out here to capture New Mexico and California, Charles would be alive.

William was angry now. First, the army had come marching right up to the fort and taken it over as if they owned it. Then they had expected him to provide food for them, to entertain the officers, to supply forage for the horses. Never mind that they were ruining the trading business, that their presence was driving the Indians away.

Then, after the army had captured New Mexico, they made Charles governor of the new American territory, but left him defenseless in Santa Fe while they marched off to California. How did they expect him to keep the natives from revolting when he had no troops?

Everything had changed. St. Vrain left the company. Got out just in time. We never saw eye to eye—it was Charles who had kept the firm together. And business kept getting worse. Still, for a while there'd been enough trading to keep the place going.

"Well, Charles is dead, and Bent, St. Vrain and Company is dead," William said aloud. "I've got a new wife and a baby on the way. I'm starting a new life. But I can't do it here with all you ghosts around, do you understand?" His voice echoed through the empty building. "I can't live here anymore. The army wants to buy the fort but won't pay me what it's worth. I can't let it fall into the hands of the Indians to use in a suicidal war against the whites. There's nothing else to do."

Swiftly he rolled the powder kegs into the main rooms. Then he set fire to the wooden roof and all the refuse that had been left behind. He had ridden half way to the camp where his family and a few employees were waiting when the powder kegs exploded.

Bent's Fort was gone.

Bent moved his family 38 miles downstream and built a new stone fort on the banks of the Arkansas River, in an area known as Big Timbers. But the second trading post was never as successful as the first had been in the 1830s, and eventually he leased it to the government.

William Bent lived for 20 years after he blew up the old fort. In that time he would see war and disease almost exterminate the Indians he loved. He would see the surge of new white settlers to this land that was once thought uninhabitable for whites. He would agonize over the fate of his four children who were trapped along Big Sandy Creek when Colonel John Chivington attacked the Indian village there. And, when they survived the massacre, he would disown one of them for murdering whites with a savagery that disgusted whites and Indians alike.

Again and again during these years William tried to bring peace between Indians and whites. He told the group of congressmen who were investigating the Sand Creek Massacre: "If the matter were left to me, I guarantee with my life that in three months I could have all the Indians along the Arkansas at peace without the expense of war." Unfortunately the US government didn't listen to William Bent.

Bent's Old Fort stands again, reconstructed by the National Park Service. A national historic site, it serves as a monument not only to Charles and William Bent, but also to the times of which they were such an important part.

*A backroad
typical of many
in Colorado*

Suggestions for Further Reading

If these tours and sketches have whetted your interest in Colorado, you may find some of the books listed below useful for broadening your knowledge about the state.

GUIDEBOOKS

Brown, Robert L. *Colorado Ghost Towns, Past and Present*. Caldwell, Idaho: Caxton Printers, 1972.

————. *Uphill Both Ways: Hiking Colorado's High Country*. Caldwell, Idaho: Caxton Printers, 1976.

Eberhart, Perry. *Guide to the Colorado Ghost Towns and Mining Camps*. 4th ed. Chicago: Swallow Press, 1968.

Grout, William. *Colorado Adventures: Forty Trips in the Rockies*. Denver: Golden Bell Press, 1974.

Hansen, Harry, and Federal Writers' Project, eds. *Colorado: A Guide to the Highest State*. Rev. ed. New York: Hastings House Publishers, 1970.

Ormes, Robert M. *Guide to the Colorado Mountains*. Rev. ed. Chicago: Swallow Press, 1970.

Parris, Lloyd. *Caves of Colorado*. Boulder, Colorado: Pruett Publishing Company, 1975.

Talmadge, Marian, and Gilmore, Iris. *Colorado Hi-Ways and By-Ways: A Comprehensive Guide to Picturesque Trails and Tours*. Boulder, Colorado: Pruett Publishing Company, 1975.

GENERAL COLORADO BOOKS

Akers, Carl. *Carl Akers' Colorado*. Fort Collins, Colorado: Old Army Press, 1975.

Busch, Paul. *Colorado Sketchbook: A Graphic History of the Early Years*. Colorado Springs: Century One Press, 1976.

Casewit, Curtis W. *Colorado*. New York: Viking, 1973.

Lavender, David. *David Lavender's Colorado*. New York: Doubleday, 1976.

Momaday, N. Scott. *Colorado*. Chicago: Rand McNally, 1973.

Wood, Myron, and Wood, Nancy C. *Colorado: Big Mountain Country*. Rev. ed. New York: Doubleday, 1972.

Worcester, Thomas K., and Pamplin, Robert B., Jr. *A Portrait of Colorado*. Beaverton, Oregon: Touchstone Press, 1976.

NATURAL HISTORY

Bailey, Alfred M., and Niedrach, Robert J. *Birds of Colorado*. 2 vols. Denver: Denver Museum of Natural History, 1965.

————. *Pictorial Checklist of Colorado Birds*. Denver: Denver Museum of Natural History, 1967.

Lechleitner, R. R. *Wild Mammals of Colorado: Their Appearance, Habits, Distribution, and Abundance*. Boulder, Colorado: Pruett Publishing Company, 1969.

Pesman, M. Walter. *Meet the Natives: An Easy Way to Recognize Wildflowers, Trees, and Shrubs of the Central Rocky Mountain Region*. 7th ed. Denver: Denver Botanic Gardens, 1967.

Weber, William A. *Rocky Mountain Flora.* 5th ed. Boulder, Colorado: Colorado Associated
University Press, 1976.

Young, Robert G., and Young, Joann W. *Geology and Wildflowers of Grand Mesa, Colorado.*
Grand Junction, Colorado: Mesa College, 1968.

Zwinger, Ann H., and Willard, Beatrice E. *Land Above the Trees: A Guide to American Alpine Tundra.*
New York: Harper and Row, 1972.

HISTORY

Abbott, Carl. *Colorado: A History of the Centennial State.* Boulder, Colorado: Colorado Associated
University Press, 1976.

Adams, Robert. *The Architecture and Art of Early Hispanic Colorado.* Boulder, Colorado:
Colorado Associated University Press, 1974.

Bird, Isabella L. *A Lady's Life in the Rocky Mountains.* The Western Frontier Library. Norman,
Oklahoma: University of Oklahoma Press, 1960.

Blair, Edward. *Palace of Ice: A History of the Leadville Ice Palace of 1896.* Leadville, Colorado:
Timberline Books, 1972.

Brown, Robert L. *Ghost Towns of the Colorado Rockies.* Caldwell, Idaho: Caxton Printers, 1968.

Colbert, Edwin H. *Men and Dinosaurs: The Search in Field and Laboratory.* New York: E. P. Dutton, 1968.

Colorado Headlines: A History of the State in Selected Newspapers of the Day. Denver: United Banks
of Colorado, 1975.

Dawson, J. Frank. *Place Names in Colorado.* Denver: Golden Bell Press, 1976.

Denver Public Library. *Nothing Is Long Ago: A Documentary History of Colorado 1776–1976.* Denver:
Denver Public Library, 1975.

Fetler, John. *The Pikes Peak People: The Story of America's Most Popular Mountain.* Caldwell, Idaho:
Caxton Printers, 1966.

Hagood, Allen. *Dinosaur: The Story Behind the Scenery.* Las Vegas: K C Publications, 1972.

Jackson, William H., and Driggs, H. R. *The Pioneer Photographer: Rocky Mountain Adventures
with a Camera.* Yonkers-on-Hudson, New York: World Book Company, 1929.

Lanham, Urless N. *The Bone Hunters.* New York: Columbia University Press, 1973.

Lavender, David. *Bent's Fort.* New York: Doubleday, 1954.

McGovern, George S., and Guttridge, Leonard F. *The Great Coalfield War.* Boston:
Houghton Mifflin, 1972.

Moore, Jackson W., Jr. *Bent's Old Fort: An Archeological Study.* Boulder, Colorado:
Pruett Publishing Company, 1973.

Neider, Charles, ed. *The Great West.* New York: Coward-McCann, 1958.

Shoemaker, Len. *Roaring Fork Valley.* 3d ed. rev. Denver: Sundance, 1973.

Sprague, Marshall. *Colorado: A Bicentennial History.* New York: W. W. Norton, 1976.

————. *A Gallery of Dudes.* Boston: Little, Brown, 1967.

————. *Massacre: The Tragedy at White River.* Boston: Little, Brown, 1957.

————. *Money Mountain: The Story of Cripple Creek Gold.* Boston: Little, Brown, 1953.

————. *One Hundred Plus: A Centennial Story of Colorado Springs.* Colorado Springs:
Colorado Springs Centennial, 1971.

Stiff, Cary. "The Dream of Dearfield." *Denver Post,* November 2, 1969, pp. 47–51.

Ubbelohde, Carl, et al. *A Colorado History: Centennial Edition.* Boulder, Colorado: Pruett
Publishing Company, 1975.

Vandenbusche, Duane, and Myers, Rex. *Marble, Colorado: City of Stone.* Denver:
Golden Bell Press, 1970.

Wolle, Muriel Sibell. *Stampede to Timberline: The Ghost Towns and Mining Camps of Colorado.*
2d rev. ed. Chicago: Swallow Press, 1974.

Wood, Mary L. *Life Against the Land: A Short History of the Pueblo Indians.* Leadville, Colorado:
Timberline Books, 1974.

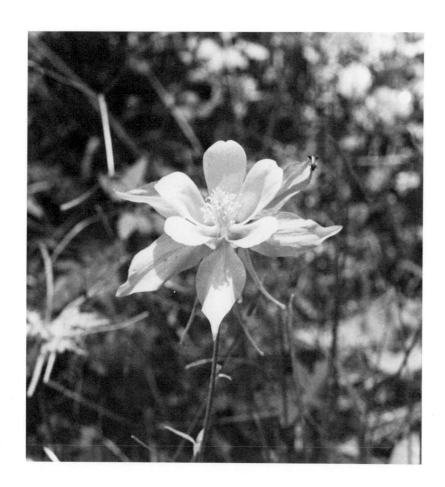

Columbine,
The State flower